Incorruptible Beauty

Incorruptible Beauty

DEPHNE MADYARA

A REVISED & UPDATED VERSION - 2017

INCORRUPTIBLE BEAUTY

Raising up warriors in a "vainglory" culture through enumerated wisdom, extricating the nuggets of beauty, valour and excellency; buried in the hearts of compromising, broken, complacent, hurt, insecure, lost, mediocre, robbed and unqualified males and females

---

Dephne Victorious Madyara

Dedication

I dedicate this book to the One I love God the Father, God the Son Jesus Christ and God the Holy Spirit. He is my Father, Shepherd and Comforter. He who has made me the woman I am today through his perfect and everlasting Love and Mercy. To Him alone be honour and glory forever and ever, Amen.

Other books written by Dephne

Breaking Soul Ties – the deliverance manual

A Woman's Body Is A Temple

A Woman's Body Is A Temple – study guide

Contents

Prologue

The Pastor at the conference had now done an altar call. My other half, a friend at the time, had invited me to a New Years Crossover Conference in London, along with his cousin sister and their friend but here I was, wrestling with God. The fear of the unknown, timidness and low self esteem had taken over and I was trying to disregard the nudge I had in my heart of walking up to the altar call by saying to myself, "maybe next time… everyone will look at me… I can't really walk all the way up there!". Are you like this today? You are making up excuses for the Holy Spirit's convictions? Are you allowing your flaws (mine at the time were fear, timidness and low self esteem) to convince you that you are not good enough for Christ, for His call and plans over your life? I spent an extensive 2-5 minutes fighting with the Holy Spirit's conviction until the other friend who had come with us interrupted my thoughts and said "do you want me to walk with you to the altar?"

Incorruptible Beauty

I don't know how she knew that I wanted to go up to the altar and give my life to Jesus Christ but I said "yes" with relief! We walked together and she left me there.

I will never forget the enigmatic sense of how clean I felt; it was un-mistakable! The supernatural power of the Holy Spirit and the joy that I felt in my heart was as if a sweeping spring of water was flushing through my mind, body and heart; minutely. Although I didn't quite understand anything about salvation but after I had said the sinner's prayer and confessed Jesus Christ as my Lord and Saviour, I knew without a doubt that I was a now a 'new person' and the old Dephne had gone.

However, within that same week of becoming saved, I had a distressing dream consecutively for 3 nights. In each of the dreams the Lord was warning me to live for Him and a huge clock would appear in the sky ticking very quickly. I didn't understand why I was having these warning dreams since I was now born again, like many Christians I believed becoming saved was my irrevocable ticket to heaven, not knowing that accepting Jesus Christ as my Saviour and Lord was just the beginning of the journey of taking up my Cross daily and following Jesus.

I needed to live for Christ and to stand by His Word by truly making Him the Master of my everyday life! For the Lord warns those that refuse to live for Him that they can lose their salvation according to the Word in Revelations 3:1-5. Sadly, because I didn't spend time discovering Jesus Christ through His Word which renews and transformed minds to confirm to Christ's way of thinking, I resorted to that which my mind was accustomed to; drunkenness, lust, selfish ambitions, lewdness and idolatry. Indeed, like a dog returns back to its own vomit, I returned back to the ways of the old Dephne; the worldly ways. However, God had mercy on me and surrounded me with good Christians who challenged me in the faith and built me up. So then, aside from the regular Sunday Church gatherings, I started attending bible and prayer meetings which enabled me to grow in the Lord. Then around 2011, I met the Lord Jesus in a vision and He touched my heart and gave me some instructions and from that moment my heart began to yearn for souls as He does. As I continued to grow in Christ, so did a burden to see souls grow out of places of stagnancy, oppression and hopelessness; I had a longing for growth in the Body of Christ.

Hence, I made a decision in my heart to serve God with all my heart and He began to teach me by His Holy Spirit that outward appearance is vanity but the inward man will live forever. I began to cultivate my inner person and through His holy Word my identity began to be formed, and even until this day He continues to open my eyes and build me up, as He also does for all His children, through His flawless Scriptures and Holy Spirit.

Similarly, the Lord Jesus is calling His people to live fully for Him, though we are evidently living in a cosmetic generation that excessively magnifies outward beauty and materialism rather than inner beauty and character. The worldly standard of living is slowly being encrypted into the Church of God resulting in lukewarm Christianity. Moreover, there's a pandemonium of fornication, adultery, emotional promiscuity, drug and alcohol abuse, gangsterism and increases in suicides amongst the youths and young adults. Christianity is being challenged everyday in a world that believes that sex is love; a generation that esteems multiple sexual partners as being qualified for romance. This then makes it difficult to live in a society that shuns the biblical principles of what a true man or woman is.

4

As a result, even the most elect Christians are being swayed and persuaded into the ways of the world. At such a time as this, when the days are fast approaching for Christ's return, there is really no more time to waste! Dear reader, are you still being swayed by the world? Still running back to your own vomit; your old ways of living? It is now time to harvest your relationship with Jesus Christ, to get up from the place of slumber and study about Jesus Christ that you may grow in Him. It's a time to commit your strength in Christ's Kingdom more than you commit it to the things of the world. Salvation is a wonderful voyage of faith and knowledge of the Person of Christ and the He desires for you to know Him. Perhaps you may have made prayers saying "Jesus I want to know You" but He is saying "I want you to know Me, draw nearer to Me!". He is wanting you to draw closer to Him and is saying "I need you and I need you desperately so that I can use your life to bring glory to My name!". Jesus is calling you not only to discover Him but to increase His Kingdom and this can only happen when you truly choose to make Him your Lord today and everyday of your life.

Incorruptible Beauty

For these reasons, this book serves to reflect inward adornment to enable recovery of sight to those blinded by the world, to rid burdens and yokes and to remove the chains of the world entangling those called and chosen by God; by imparting Godly wisdom, strength, knowledge, virtue and etiquette of true Incorruptible Beauty that is founded on the Word of God. For it is the Word of God and the Blood of Jesus that expose sin and bring deliverance. Correspondingly, in this book you will become equipped by knowing what a man is and God's plan for men. You will understand what a woman is, her beauty and role on earth. You will be able to discern the truth and gain wisdom on subjects such as love, sex and relationships and to know what God's standard is on these subjects as compared to the world's standard. Moreover, as every human being is uniquely gifted and has a bright future, you will also learn about destiny killers such as the spirit of Jezebel, Athaliah and Delilah which seek to terminate one's gifts, anointing or future.

Therefore, my prayer for you is that you will begin to see what a great man or woman you are, and are destined to be, and that you may come to the revelation of knowing and experiencing the Power of Christ's enduring Love and

Mercy, so that your identity is completely conformed to His perfect Will, in the name of Jesus the Christ, Amen.

Chapter One

MAN

What do you think describes a fine man? Is it his 6 pack muscles, his swell bank balance or charisma? When Jesus Christ asked His disciples in Matthew 16:15 saying "who do the crowds say that I am?" Those crowds because they didn't walk with Him to be able to know Him, they thought He was John the Baptist, some thought prophet Elijah, still others said He was Jeremiah or one of the prophets. Upon asking this same question to His disciples who walked with Him and knew Him, Peter answered by the unction and revelation of the Holy Spirit that Jesus was the Messiah, the Son of the living God. It was the Holy Spirit speaking through Peter who knew who Jesus was because He, the Spirit of God has been there from the beginning. It is the same with a man, you may have many descriptions for what a man is, but it is God who created and envisioned a man. Hence, through the Holy Scriptures we can attain knowledge of the full identity of a man. By the end of this chapter you will begin to understand what a man is and know what his role on earth is according to God's design and will.

Introduction

In Genesis 1:26-27 it's written, *"Then God said, "Let Us make man in Our image, according to Our likeness; let them have dominion over the fish of the sea, over the birds of the air, and over the cattle, over all the earth and over every creeping thing that creeps on the earth." So God created man in His own image; in the image of God He created him; male and female He created them."* Mankind is created in God's 'Image' meaning we look like God, hence, men and women alike are made in God's image. So what does God Almighty look like? Well beloved, He looks like you and me. John 4:24 says *"God is Spirit, and those who worship Him must worship in spirit and truth."* Therefore you being made in His image means you are also a spirit being. Of all God's creatures we mankind alone are like Him rationally, wilfully and being capable of making moral choices.

We are also created after his 'Likeness', meaning that we were created to function like God in word, deed and action.

To reflect His beauty, righteousness, holiness, wisdom and glory upon the earth which He made for us mankind as it says in Psalm 115:16 *"The heaven, even the heavens, are the LORD's; but the earth He has given to the children of men."* In this manner, men and women were both given dominion over the earth. God made both the man and woman to share equally in His image, likeness and dominion in the earth as it is written in Genesis 1:26, *"let them have dominion over the fish of the sea, over the birds of the air, and over every creeping thing that creeps on earth."* This is because in the spiritual realm there is no gender. Hence, it is important that you grasp the differences between the physical realm and the spiritual realm because in the physical realm there are differences of roles between a man and a woman yet spiritually they are the same.

Moreover, everything God does or says first goes and occupies the spirit realm before it manifests to the physical realm. This is demonstrated during the creation process all throughout Genesis chapter 1, when God would speak something and it was so. He would envisage what He wanted to make spiritually and it would manifest in the physical realm as such.

However in chapter 2 we see a different picture showing the physical realm and the order of how creation was made is not the same as in chapter 1. For example, in chapter 1 of Genesis 1:24-28 which shows the spiritual realm, the beasts of the field were made first and then mankind; both on the sixth day. However, in chapter 2 which shows the physical realm, the man is physically made first and then the beasts of the field (compare Genesis 2:7 and 2:18-20). This is because there is a spiritual realm and a physical realm, and it is God who determines the manifestation of each because He ordained time and seasons both spiritually and physically. God has told you something but you are not yet seeing its manifestation in your life? Do not worry because there is a time and season ordained for that thing God told you, to manifest accordingly. Just continue to have faith and trust in the Lord despite what you are physically seeing today.

Therefore, considering these differences between the spiritual and physical realms, there is also however, a further point to be considered.

Before a man was physically created, God had spoken a covenant blessing into his spirit together with his wife according to Genesis 1:28 saying to them *"be fruitful and multiply; fill the earth and subdue it; have dominion over the fish of the sea, over the birds of the air, and over every living thing that moves on earth"*. This is a spiritual blessing and command that cannot be grasped nor fully experienced if God the One who blesses is not included in the marriage union or individual lives of a man and a woman. A married man and his wife have to die to self daily in order to invite God into their marriage. That is to mean, dying daily to their own selfish wants in order to welcome and accommodate God's mandate and blessing for their lives and marriage; walking in His Word. It can be difficult to consciously invite GOD in a marriage covenant and observe the divine biblical order of marriage, when one did not learn to do so in their premarital stages of life.

Hence, it is important to continuously invite God into your individual life in order to be able to invite God in a future marriage equation as Psalms 127:1 says, *"Unless the LORD builds the house, the builders labour in vain..."*. Indeed, they that build a house, build it in vain if the LORD does not build it.

13

There can be serious problems when one does not invite God in their personal life daily because consequently, it is possible for two Christians to be married but the wife behaving in a Jezebelic manner and the husband behaving in an Ahab manner, to the non-fulfilment of the dominion mandate. The dominion mandate being, Christ is the head of the husband and the husband is the head of the wife. The marriage blessing spoken by God to the first marriage couple still has power to work in every 21st century married couple in Christ. However, when order is broken, there is disorder and when the order of God concerning marriage is broken, there are disastrous consequences. For example, when a man does not take his role and responsibility in the home, it leaves a vacuum for Satan to fill with worldly wisdom and desires. For this reason, Satan is after the head of the home - men! Hence, he fights one of the biggest threat which overcomes him and that threat is marriage (the union of a man and a woman).

So then, Satan tries to manipulate this order of marriage by fighting young men before they marry. Satan gets them while they are still young to get them off-track.

He influences them with worldly wisdom on play station games, sex, material wealth, pornography, popular gadgets and secular music. His aim is to stimulate obsession which in turn births idolatry and sin, such that their actions become poisoned in order to repel the favour of God over their lives instead of attracting it. It is very important that as Christians we pray for all males out there, no matter the age group because these prayers will save many men from a destructive destiny.

The Creation Process of A Man

At creation God made the man first before the woman as it says in Genesis 2:7 (NIV) "***And the LORD God formed man of the dust of the ground, and breathed into his nostrils the breath of life; and man became a living soul.***" Indeed, just as a potter forms his pottery, the Lord God formed Adam in God's image. The compelling nature of his forming is that the Hebrew word used for "of the dust" is Aphar, which means rubbish/mortar/ashes. Hence, the man was formed from the rubbish, ashes and mortar of the earth into God's image but inside him was hidden something unique; his rib. Therefore, each man who has been called for marriage has his wife hidden in him and he need not look far to find her. The Holy Spirit will lead him to where he needs to be (whether it's physically, spiritually or emotionally) in order to identify and receive his wife tangibly.

Now, when Adam was fully formed and whole, he immediately took on the role of covering his wife. He covered her while she hid in his side as a rib. In that season of Adam's life, he covered Eve physically though not as yet bodily until she showed up tangibly.

16

For this reason, a man ought to keep himself chaste as he waits for his wife to be tangibly presented to him for marriage. Sadly, the enemy blinds the men of this society by enticing them to walk in the ways of fornication and multiple romantic relationships. They are deceived by the devil's 21st century propaganda into thinking that walking in these ways somehow attributes men to masculinity, intellectuality and strength. Unfortunately, by the time a wife is presented to the man who walked in the paths of fornication and multiple romantic relationships, he is damaged emotionally, physically or spiritually and is unable to fully yield and cleave (emotionally, sexually, financially and spiritually) to his wife as he should until he receives God's healing and deliverance. Dear reader, have you walked in fornication but now want to leave that way of living? The only begotten son of God, Jesus Christ gave His life for you and all who would believe in Him by dying on the Cross for your sins and rising up after 3 days. You can receive His forgiveness today when you confess to Him your sin. Will you repent today from fornication and trust God's enabling power to help you overcome the cowardice lifestyle of multiple relationships and fornication?

Receive His deliverance and healing as you live a lifestyle of repentance, clothing yourself daily with Christ and trusting Him alone to make you whole for your covenant spouse. (See the prayer at the end of this chapter)

By the same token, after forming Adam, God breathed into Adam's nostrils the breath of life, meaning that the very life of God came into the man and he became a living soul who functions in the likeness of God. Interestingly enough, Jesus demonstrates this very act to his disciples in John 20:22 which says, ***"And when He had said this, He breathed on them, and said to them, "Receive the Holy Spirit."***

Therefore, we ought to know by this that Adam became filled with the Holy Spirit and since his wife was hidden in him, she too became filled (today each person is filled through salvation in Christ and by faith). Unfortunately, whether a man knows God or not, when he is called to marriage, he will play the role of covering his wife according to his understanding, whether in love or in hate; with wisdom or with folly. He is wired this way from the creation of man whether he knows God or not.

Indeed, as a covering, he will yearn to lead, to be respected, to be listened to, to be admired and be cheered on whether he is poor, rich, sick, healthy, handsome, unattractive, romantic or unromantic. A man's selfhood and rapport is articulately designed in such a way because of how God created man along with his role of headship and covering according to God's way. For these reasons, every man needs God to walk in his full capacity and believe you me, a shrink, hypnotist or counsellor won't be as good as God, God's Word and God's Spirit. Surely, a man will need daily fellowship with God because God is the Author and Perfecter of his life as it's written, "***Therefore we also, since we are surrounded by so great a cloud of witnesses, let us lay aside every weight, and the sin which so easily ensnares us, and let us run with endurance the race that is set before us, looking unto Jesus, the author and finisher of our faith, who for the joy that was set before Him endured the cross, despising the shame, and has sat down at the right hand of the throne of God.***"

Finally, as the first man Adam opened his eyes after being formed, he beheld the glory of his Creator and reflected that glory upon the earth because he was clothed in it.

The first voice he heard was the voice of God which spoke tenderly to him, a voice that delighted in him. Undoubtedly, man is God's greatest creation and masterpiece because he is the image and glory of God (see 1 Corinthians 11:7). Man was created to know God, for it's written in John 17:3, "**And this is eternal life, that they may know You, the only true God, and Jesus Christ whom You have sent.**" And to have fellowship with God on earth and for eternity as it says in 2 Corinthians 13:14 (NIV), "**May the grace of the Lord Jesus Christ, and the love of God, and the fellowship of the Holy Spirit be with you all**".

Sadly, now with an increasing trend of eristical and delusional feminist movements, this further blinds the eyes of society from the true picture of what a man should be along with his responsibilities. Godly insight into why God made a man to have so much responsibility is vital in this society because it's evident that without God's character instilled inside a man, he is inevitably bound to lose at life by returning to the characteristics of mortar, ashes and rubbish. Therefore, the God who formed man, is the only One who is able to sustain and hold him up by His Spirit to be conformed to the character and mind of Christ.

Dephne Madyara

Only in God does a man truly know who he is and his purpose upon the earth. For instance, if you put a fish in water its genius emerges but when you take it out it suffocates and dies. Likewise, in the presence of God a man flourishes in spirit, soul and body.

The Role of A Man

In a generation that has seen a great rise in women's groups crying for their women's rights and some of these rights removing the man from his rightful place and role, to the extent that some women say "Girl you don't need a man, who needs them or we can live without them". All these things reflect how this generation can no longer recognise that when God's order spoken in 1 Corinthians 11.3, "***But there is one thing I want you to know: The head of every man is Christ, the head of woman is man, and the head of Christ is God***", is broken, there is disorder affecting families and their future generations! This is exactly what the enemy wants, to distort God's marital and family order. Distortion of God's marital and family order has opened a dangerous vacuum for poverty, gangsterism, selling or using drugs, prostitution, abuse, premarital sex, divorce, witchcraft and many other issues to sweep into individual's lives.

Noting the compelling nature of this, in order to really understand the role of a man, we would need to go back to the bible; the beginning in Genesis 1 and 2. These chapters show God's original purpose for man.

When Jesus Christ was being questioned about marriage and divorce in Matthew 19:3-9, He referred to Genesis 2:24 by saying, "*The Pharisees also came to Him, testing Him, and saying to Him, "Is it lawful for a man to divorce his wife for just any reason?" And He answered and said to them, "Have you not read that He who made them at the beginning 'made them male and female,'and said, 'For this reason a man shall leave his father and mother and be joined to his wife, and the two shall become one flesh'? So then, they are no longer two but one flesh. Therefore what God has joined together, let not man separate." They said to Him, "Why then did Moses command to give a certificate of divorce, and to put her away?" He said to them, "Moses, because of the hardness of your hearts, permitted you to divorce your wives, but from the beginning it was not so. And I say to you, whoever divorces his wife, except for sexual immorality, and marries another, commits adultery; and whoever marries her who is divorced commits adultery."*"

From that passage of scripture, we see how the Pharisees referred to Moses, but Jesus went way past Moses to the beginning, likewise in order for us to really understand the role of a man, let's go past what mama said, what daddy said, what the home-boys or home-girls say and what Hollywood says and go to what God says! The characteristics of the role of a man are depicted in the book of Genesis 2 and are as follows:-

A man who loves God and His presence

Adam knew the presence and atmosphere of God and was acquainted with God before he knew a woman and started a family. The problem we have in today's society is that men start a family then they know a woman (marriage) and then, in some instances, they become acquintained with God later on in life, hence, the order God purposed for man is being broken. The Lord wants to make Himself known to men and help them come to the realisation that only in His presence does their soul find satisfaction. God wants them to understand that they were created to know, be and live in His presence. Dear reader, are you living in God's presence today?

When you are not in His presence, there is always a deep longing within. Indeed, you will always be searching and trying to satisfy this longing and you may find yourself thinking or saying things like "there is something missing in my life". Have you been saying that to yourself or feeling this way? Feeling that there is a void and something is missing? It's the presence of God missing in your life. It's not the money, sex, drugs nor alcohol that can fill this void but daily fellowship with God.

God desires for men to seek Him even in their loneliest and darkest nights, crying out to Him without shame for His helping hand, instead of looking for comfort to release frustration through drugs, binge drinking, binge eating, clubbing, gangs, sinful sex and pornography. Those things may paint a masterpiece Picasso for a "solution", yet the solution always proves temporary! It just never takes away the void, emptiness or pain permanently. When the 4 hours of clubbing, dancing and lifting up hands to secular music artists are over, the pain comes back again. When the 20 minutes of sex is over and your lover is gone, the loneliness comes back again. When the alcohol or drugs wear out, the sorrow comes back again. All those things just never suffice!

Dear reader, are you looking for comfort through temporary pleasures of the world? In your search for peace and joy, are you getting addicted to things that can slowly kill or destroy you? The fleeting pleasures of life can never bring lasting change into our hearts and lives. Only the resurrection life in Christ can bring total healing and liberty.

It is written in Genesis 2:8, ***"The LORD God planted a garden eastward in Eden, and there He put the man whom He had formed"***. Then Hebrew word for Eden is "`EDEN"` which means "*pleasure, delight*". Eden was more than just a place on earth, it was an atmosphere and realm where God Almighty would meet with mankind. No wonder why it's called pleasant and delight! It's the present fellowship of God that made it so! Indeed, in God's presence there is no lack of unprecedented delight. Do you have a meeting place with God? Have you mastered the privilege you have in Christ of going boldly to the throne of grace, that you may obtain mercy and find grace to help you in your time of need? Apostle Paul says in Colossians 4:2 (NLT) ***"devote yourselves to prayer, with an alert mind and a thankful heart"***.

The man who always prays will *always* find delight and pleasantness because having a daily meeting place with God in your life will bring an atmosphere of pleasantness and delight in your daily life. Surely the sorrows, worries and cares of this world will have no ruler-ship over those who delight in the Lord at all times and they will find strength to overcome the daily sorrows of this life and world.

A man who works

Genesis 2:15 (KJV) says, "***and the LORD God took the man and put him in the Garden of Eden to dress and to keep it***". The Hebrew word used for dress is "`ABAD" which means "*to work, to serve by labour*", and the Hebrew word used for keep is "SHAMAR" which means "*to keep, treasure up, guard, observe and give heed*". There is great coherence to the responsibility God gave the man. He was to work and serve that which God had given him in that season of his life; the garden of Eden in this case.

Likewise, the role of the man is to work and be a provider. For if the man Adam could not work and labour for the garden by keeping it, treasuring it, guarding it, observing and giving heed to it, how would he keep, treasure, guard, observe and give heed to his wife and children? Adam needed a season of working as a single man so that he can be skilled to perform and apply those same principles towards his wife and family in the seasons of marital partnership and fatherhood. Dear reader, God is a lover of working! He Himself worked for six days when He created the heavens, the earth and all the host of them, then He rested on the seventh day. Throughout the book of Proverbs, the bible discourages laziness and in 2 Thessalonians 3:10 (NKJV) it says, ***"For even when we were with you, we commanded you this: If anyone will not work, neither shall he eat."***

Now, in our generation the dynamics of work in gender roles have changed after the 2nd World War, whereby in those days men went to war leaving the women and children at home and as the war intensified women were brought to work in factories making weaponry; predominately working in roles that were traditionally filled by men. Today in this 21st century, we now see how this has birthed a new revolution of both men and women working. Moreover, between the 1960's and 1970's an Equal Pay Act was introduced in most first world countries which meant that it was illegal to pay men and women different wages because it made no sense to pay the one more than the other based on gender, since the job required equal skills, effort and was performed under similar working conditions. Despite all these changes that have occurred over the millenniums to this present generation, it is important for both men and women to know that the man still ought to work and walk fully in his role of being a provider as demonstrated in Genesis 2:15, "***Then the Lord God took the man and put him in the garden of Eden to tend and keep it.***" For, before Adam received Eve in the flesh, whilst she was still hidden in him, Adam was given a garden and a task by God and at that very commission he became his wife's financial covering. Therefore, men ought not to squander their money on different women or fruitless things but a man must use wisdom to save and create a financial reservoir that he can use in marriage as he demonstrates the role of being a provider whilst building a family with his wife.

This is God's original plan and dynamic before sin entered the world, for men to be providers through God's provision and their labour of it. Unfortunately, the world and its systems are now grooming men and women otherwise; couples turn away from doing it God's way into doing it "their way". The influences of today's modern culture makes it increasingly difficulty for a man to be a man in this society.

According to the National UK Statistics in 2012, it has been proven that men are 3 times more likely to commit suicide than women. This is alleged to be based on financial conflictions. Moreover, some husbands who have contentious wives have fallen into great debt and financial turmoils by being influenced to keep up with the Joneses or play a conspicuous role of 'Provider'. Other husbands have wise wives but due to the great responsibility they need to walk in, instead of turning to God for strength, some have turned to addictions and strange practices to ease the pressure of being a Provider. For these reasons, it is only God who formed the man who can help a man to be a man, a husband and/or a father. It is God who sustains, strengthens and helps him to be all that he was created to be because man *cannot* do life on his own without God.

He cannot victoriously play the role of 'being a man' with human strength and wisdom. Therefore, though times have changed, God's Word still remains the same and His Word still requires a man to be a provider and God is able to provide the grace and power to men whether single or married to be financially successful.

A man who knows the Word of God

Many men in our generation have been deceived into thinking that passion for the Word of God and things of God should be spearheaded by women. For example, it is common to see a mother on an early Sunday morning getting the children ready for church, while the husband sits on the sofa with the remote control flipping through the channels for the next football match saying to the wife "pray for me today!". This ought not to be so, rather the man is the one who is meant to be more zealous and equipped with Word of God in order to accomplish God's plan written in Ephesians 5:25-26, *"Husbands, love your wives, just as Christ also loved the church and gave Himself for her, that He might sanctify and cleanse her with the washing of water by the word"*.

A man was meant to be filled with God's Word that he may effectively admonish, teach and equip his home, family and environment while glorifying God in image and likeness. It's so important that a man be filled with so much knowledge of God's Word because without knowledge of God's Word and counsel from the Holy Spirit, a married man can easily begin to rule over his wife rather than leading her.

After the fall of mankind it is written in Genesis 3:16, ***"To the woman He said: "I will greatly multiply your sorrow and your conception; in pain you shall bring forth children; Your desire shall be for your husband, and he shall rule over you."'*** God never intended for a husband to rule over his wife. Please understand that there is no joint partnership when one rules over the other. Kings rule over kingdoms, a government rules over a country, bosses rule over companies; all those under their care are as subjects and not as partners. The partnership blessing of headship was taken away when Adam conceded to his wife's voice instead of God's voice by not exercising his role of "covering" Eve from the devil who had tempted her to disobey God's command; Adam's compliance in this sin took away the blessing of headship replacing it with rulership.

After Adam and Eve sinned, the harmonious dynamics of marriage (God being head of the husband and the husband being head of the wife) were broken through Adam's act of eating the forbidden fruit. When Eve convinced her husband Adam to eat the fruit that God had told him not to eat, this was a demonstration of exerting authority over him and a reflection of the desire to take on his role of leader.

Visually, this act painted a picture of Eve being the head of Adam and Adam being the head of God through disobeying God's command. The enemy completely reversed God's structure mandate of marriage through sin as illustrated below:

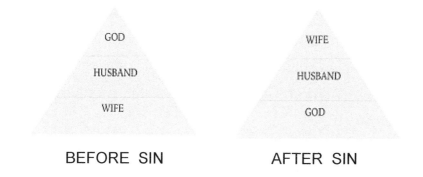

BEFORE SIN   AFTER SIN

As a result, the husband who operates under the curse of sin can only work the through the broken dynamics of marriage by exercising torrid mastery in order to keep his place of headship when his wife desires to dominate him through her actions and words. This power struggle is a mindset of the fallen nature which can only be overcome by both spouses renewing their minds with God's word in order to walk daily in God's true dynamics of marriage. The dynamics rooted in a man should be to lead his wife as God leads Him (Ephesians 5:23); to leave (not isolate) father and mother and cleave to his wife (Genesis 2:24); and lastly to love his wife as Christ loves the Church (Ephesians 5:25).

Indeed, there is no rulership in the partnership of marriage when a man operates under the true knowledge of headship and leadership. For the wife the dynamics rooted in her ought to be that she does not desire her husband's place but rather she submits to him as unto Jesus her Lord (Ephesians 5:22) and she respects him (Ephesians 5:33).

Unfortunately, some wives today who are saved by grace, still desire to control their husbands in certain areas of their marriage and as a result the husband rises up to rule over his wife instead of leading her because the opportunity to lead is made fragile and narrow. It is only the "*revelation*" of Jesus Christ that brings balance for a man and a woman in a committed relationship. Without revelation of the Truth, the mind of a man will become depraved of wisdom and will automatically adopt to the standard of "**he will rule over you**". It is a tragedy when a man, instead of ruling over sin and Satan, he begins to be idle by operating with a dictatorship attitude and character, vainly thinking that this so called 'boldness' is a demonstration of being a man. Through the Blood and Water (salvation and revelation of Jesus Christ) this curse is overcome! It's important for men to have a daily relationship with Jesus Christ and to have a daily bible study time to fill the mind with God's Word in order to overcome situations that will cause them to operate under the fallen nature.

Therefore, it's vital for a man to know and have revelation of God's word and character, understanding that in Christ a man and a woman are now equal spiritually, as both have king-ship in Christ and are priests, for it's written in Galatians 3:28, "*There is neither Jew nor Greek, there is neither slave nor free, there is neither male nor female; for you are all one in Christ Jesus.*" Moreover, being equipped through the Word of God in order to walk in the different roles of a man and a woman physically, that in marriage the man is the head of the home as it is written in 1 Corinthians 11.3, "*But there is one thing I want you to know: The head of every man is Christ, the head of woman is man, and the head of Christ is God.*" I would remind you that anything with two heads is a monster; there can only be one head in a marriage and that is the husband!

A man who is a cultivator

Though Christ is the head of the Church, He still serves the church though He is above her (see Romans 8:34). Christ Jesus still serves all His children (His Bride) in humility, watching diligently over her for opposing dangers, tending to her cares, mistakes and weaknesses; and giving heed to her yearnings both in seasons of joy and pain by His Spirit.

Hence, the man also ought to do likewise because this same grace of humility and love has also been placed in men. Men were given this great honour of valour, to be cultivators!

A cultivator is a leader and visionary. Men are given the responsibility to make final decisions because of the vision dynamically installed in their minds and hearts; this is why Satan hates men. He envies their duty and is frantically fighting men all over the world by altering their places of cultivation but thanks be to God who by His Holy Spirit has power to navigate a man's eyes and hands (his vision and strength). Many men are weak nowadays because they are using their strength on fruitless deeds. Many men are visually impaired and cannot see where they are going in life because they don't use God's Word to be a light unto their road. The Holy Spirit Power of God is the Teacher, Comforter, Counsellor, Advocate and Helper; He is the One who reminds, empowers, gives wisdom, encourages and consequently shows a man how to cultivate, where to cultivate and what to cultivate.

Incorruptible Beauty

It's through a relationship with the Holy Spirit transfigured in God's Word and without the Holy Spirit of God, a man's vision is darkened and he will automatically start cultivating, nourishing and nurturing the things of darkness which are rebellion and sin. In the very Body of Christ today, we are now face a deficit of God willed cultivators because many men are cultivating the wrong things.

Moreover, not only is the man a cultivator in the things of life, for example, social and business endeavours whereby he reflects the glory of God in his businesses, friendships, ministry, workplace or education but also more importantly, he is meant to be a cultivator to his wife. To nurture her and nourish her, to protect her, to help bring out her beauty in the same way Christ does to the Church. For the young men to be cultivators in their behaviour towards the opposite sex by not trying uncover the nakedness of their sister in Christ through lust. Sadly, we now live in a society where media encourages and accepts the behaviours of men who are thieves and terrorists to women. Young men who lie their way through by making false promises of marriage, giving many material things or wearing a prince charming mask in order to gain sexual favours.

Evidently, a man walking in wisdom cannot want sex from a woman who is not his wife and be puffed up about it, professing out loudly this shame as "I'm a man!" or "I'm the man!". Indeed, only a fool can have illicit sex with different women, and because he doesn't realise that he is giving away his strength to them; he all the more walks around boasting about his so called endeavours. I want you to know that it takes a fool to do such things, for no wise man can be proud of cultivating sin and rebellion. The lack of God's knowledge and wisdom in a believer's life causes them to be like a fool by behaving rebelliously, as it is written in Proverbs 10:23, "*to do evil is like a sport to a fool but a man of understanding has wisdom*". Wisdom and knowledge is found in God's Word.

Evaluation

Now do you can see what God's plan for a man is and how his character ought to exhibit that of the LORD Jesus? For when God spoke in Now do you can see what God's plan for a man is and how his character ought to exhibit that of the LORD Jesus? For when God spoke in Genesis 2:18, "**Now the Lord God said, It is not good (sufficient, satisfactory) that the man should be alone; I will make him a helper meet (suitable, adapted, complementary) for him.**" He wasn't talking to an ordinary man but speaking to a man acquainted with His presence and Word, a man who loved and reverenced Him, a man who was able to be a cultivator and nurturer through the Holy Spirit of God. For this reason, men ought to serve God and not Satan any longer through the fruitless deeds of the world. It's time for men to begin to lay aside the ways of the world and put on Jesus Christ the True image of a Man. It's time for men to begin severing out every idolatry and rebellion out of their lives. Perhaps, you are the one that needs to do this today?

It's a choice you can make today and this choice wont take more than 5 minutes to decide that you want to change, that you want God to have full access and control of what you look at, listen to and speak, because these things are the core influencers of actions. It's time to begin to learn how to test what you listen to before they let it into your heart. It's time to absorb the true and living strength, motivation, armour and delight that springs forth from the living Word of God. By disposing testimonies and sermons that come from reckless and lost souls living on the edge who call them selves Hip-Hop, R&B, Rap and Rock Superstars. A man is not receiving any edification in his life by constantly absorbing words like "I want to take you to bed", or "I want to make love on the dance-floor", or "lets smoke that weed tonight". This is in-fact trains and builds strongholds of rebellion in his mind. Such a man becomes what he hears because what he's hearing is being processed in his thoughts and these thoughts manifest into feelings and actions.

Today can be the start of no longer pursuing strength through various contaminations but to pursue Christ Jesus the true source of strength.

Incorruptible Beauty

The strength of a man is not found in his pride but in his humility, just like with Christ. Men are being taught by society that boldness is evidenced through being rogue and proud, but this is a lie, for boldness is found in Christ through love, integrity and humility. The time has come for men to be all that God has called them out to be. To put away the pollution they listen to on billboards music charts and start listening to God through His Word.

Jesus is the Restorer of Breaches. He is the Friend who sticks closer than a brother. He is the only One who takes away the pain, sorrow, grief and loneliness permanently. He has given those who believe in Him, His Holy Spirit to comfort and help in those hard times when facing the storms of this life. Hope and Comfort is found in Jesus for those who need it. All you have to do is ask Him. The Holy Spirit Power of God will counsel you when your body cannot handle its sexual cravings any longer, when your family and friends reject you; and when you feel hopeless and need direction and inspiration. Now before you ask God and kneel before Him to pray this prayer below, begin to tell Jesus how you feel, tell Him all your pain and everything that you have been hiding. Begin to open up your heart to Him exposing yourself to Him.

This will quicken your healing process. Remember, there is no use in hiding anything from Him or being ashamed because He already knew everything about you and wrote in His book every mistake you would make even before you were born, for it is written in Psalm 139:16 (GW), *"Your eyes saw me when I was still an unborn child. Every day of my life was recorded in Your book before one of them had taken place."*

Prayer

Jesus the Author and Perfecter of my faith; I lay aside my pride, my mask, my selfish needs and wants, my garments of shame at Your feet LORD asking You to make me realise and be the man you want me to be and created me to be. Forgive me of my sins and strengthen me in my weaknesses (name all the weaknesses that you need Jesus to deliver you from). Heal my insecurities (name them) and take away my burdens and reproaches LORD Jesus. Build me up with Your love and might; and fill me today with Your Holy Spirit, that I may function like You in such a time as this. I thank You Jesus for hearing and answering my prayer, in Jesus Name, AMEN. (If you are a woman reading this, you can begin to pray the things you have learnt in this chapter over your husband, sons, future husband or future sons).

Practical Action Plan

The "Practical Side" of this Prayer is to now fill your mind with the Scriptures. Let the Word of God always be in you so as to walk in it, by studying it daily, for it is written in Psalms 1: 1-3 (AMP) "**BLESSED (happy, fortunate, prosperous, and enviable) is the man who walks and lives not in the counsel of the ungodly [following their advice, their plans and purposes], nor stands [submissive and inactive] in the path where sinners walk, nor sits down [to relax and rest] where the scornful [and the mockers] gather. But his delight and desire are in the law of the LORD, and on His law (the precepts, the instructions, the teachings of God) he habitually meditates (ponders and studies) by day and by night. And he shall be like a tree firmly planted [and tended] by the streams of water, ready to bring forth its fruit in its season; its leaf also shall not fade or wither; and everything he does shall prosper [and come to maturity].**"

Another significant factor is to look at the things that you are giving your time to and decide if they are worth your efforts in the long run.

Decide by multiplying this thing you give your time to by 100. Is it an investment or a hazardous debt to your future? Because surely pornography, violent video games, horror films, gangster films, bad friends and sexually lyricist songs are eating away any value in you and in your life. They will definitely be like an acid to your future. Today you can make a decision to put a stop to all the toxic things that you allow daily to flow freely your life and replace those things with studying the Word of God, accompanying it with prayer that you may stand upright and stand fast armed as a warrior being equipped like the man of God that you are meant to be! Amen.

Dephne Madyara

CHAPTER TWO

WOMAN

Dephne Madyara

What is a woman, is it her 36 inch hips, 24 inch waist or 36 inch bust? What is it that makes her beautiful, is it the tone of her skin or texture of her hair? I'm saddened by how the world is raising up empty cylinders plastered with good-looks. I'm sorry that Hollywood testifies that your look is all you need to walk up the mountain of life, they lied! There's more to you than the shape of your body, there's more to you than your envied full lips, there's more to you than those pretty eyes and cheek bones you have, other's more to you than you clothing and shoe collection. Yes, there's a great deal more to a woman than her outward appearance. When God fearfully and wonderfully made her, this mystery went beyond her physique, intellectual and sexuality. What does God say about a woman? After all, it is God who formed and built her. In this chapter it will be revealed to you what a woman is through God's Word and by the end of this chapter you will know what a woman is; her character, excellence, beauty, mission and role on earth.

Introduction

We live in a world that celebrates women for their physical appearance more than their character, intellectuality, moral compass and life. The true nature and will of a woman's identity is gradually becoming lost in the scrambles of social, economic and cultural outlooks. Now more than ever, there's a need for women to fight the world's influences that try to define daily who they are; women have to believe and stand on God's Word in order to keep God's standards because it is God who envisioned and created them, not society. Therefore, it's imperative that both men and women go back to the genesis of God's original plan in order to understand what and who a woman is because God's original plan for creating the first woman is a resourceful map for every other woman who came after her. In Genesis 2:18, God introduces us to the first woman based on the plan He had for the first man when He said, **"It is not good that man should be alone; I will make him a helper comparable to him."** The Hebrew word used for "helper" is 'EZER which means Helper/ One who helps/ Succor (succor means help; relief; aid; assistance).

So then, the first lesson we learn about a woman of God is that she was created to be a helper to her husband within the life long specification of their marriage. In short, a woman was created to be a wife! Have you ever wondered why so many single women crave for marriage? Have you ever considered why little girls begin to plan their wedding day in their heads gasping at the idea of their wedding dress? Although society is irked by such marriage idioms in millions of females all over the world, unfortunately, these instincts are within women and are not by chance; they are inevitable because of how God formed and fashioned the female being; God designed her with marriage in mind. Therefore, it's healthy to desire marriage as a single woman but it is unhealthy to obsess over marriage. Never the less, some may say that not every woman is created to be a wife. Rightly so, however, God's plan for creating a woman was so that she can be a wife - a helper. The bible says in 1 Corinthians 11:8-9, *"for man is not from woman, but woman from man. Nor was man created for the woman, but woman for man."*

So, whether a woman chooses not to get married according to 1 Corinthians 7:8, she is not sinning by choosing that path and if God tells her not to get married, that is up to her and God.

Thus, the woman was fashioned from the man's side for the conclusive purpose of making that man's life, from whose side she taken from, better. She betters his life through her help, relief, aid and assistance; emotionally, financially, intellectually, physically, psychologically, sexually and spiritually. Please understand from this that according to God's spoken Word, the woman is to help her husband in all these areas; not her male acquaintance, boyfriend, fiancé nor pastor. The problems we face today both in the Church and Society are that helpers (women) are trying to play the role of helper outside marriage and/or helpers are not equipped (spiritually, mentally and emotionally) enough to be helpers to their own husbands at home. The full role of being a helpmeet flourishes when accomplished within the correct specifications. Are you a woman today playing the role of a helper to someone who is not yet your husband? Perhaps you are giving away all your intellectual virtues to a man who is not yet your husband?

Don't use your powerful role of being a helper prematurely. This is why the path of multiple dating/relationships always poses a risk to one's virtues stored up for their future spouse. For instance, if you are a woman dating different men every few months in search of your husband, you can fall into the danger of investing your intellectual, spiritual and emotional strengths in relationships and people whom you have no future with. Eventually this can take its toll on you in some aspect and rob you from giving 100% of your mind and heart to your true life long mate especially if the previous relationships concluded on fear or broken trust.

Therefore, whenever you and I try to outsmart God by improvising our own ideas and plans over God's way of doing things, there is always a result of limitation or err. A woman was not created to help, relieve and aid a man who is not her husband the way she should towards a husband. A woman cannot be a financial aid to a man who is not her husband and still expect to him to play a conspicuous role of leading her.

A woman who gives husband privileges (spiritually, emotionally, physically or sexually) to a man who is not her husband puts herself and her future husband in great deficit! This robs the marriage bank of their future marriage. God's blessings founded on the role of being helpmate reside within marriage; outside marriage, this role only produces toiling, confusion and disappointments. Are you relieving your so called "boyfriend" sexually in the hopes that he will quickly respond back to you with an engagement ring or marriage? He seems to know how to express to you his need for your sexual help but he can't lawfully express by right of marriage his commitment to you before God and people? Don't allow the devil to convince you that being a helpmate to someone who is not your husband will bring blessings and fast results because it won't; it's a deception of the devil. When a woman tries to play the role of "helper" to a man who is not yet her husband, she will eventually become tired, frustrated and angry as she realises that he is not responding back to her. A fiancé or boyfriend is not in a positioned to respond back from the position of "husband" because that is not his role in her life; it is only a husband who positioned to respond back to her as his wife.

More importantly, a husband who is spiritually awakened through faith in the LORD Jesus Christ and has daily fellowship with the Spirit of God; such a man is fully adapted to respond daily towards his wife through his husbanding attributes and abilities. Again, I say a husband led daily by the Spirit of God because it is very possible for a wife to do everything in her virtuous ability to help her saved and sanctified husband but unless her saved and sanctified husband has an active daily relationship with God, he may not understand that his wife is his helper in every aspect of his life nor see how she is helping him. In such cases, her virtuous work may go unnoticed or worse, she and her works may face forms of rejection.

Comparatively, the bible gives us insight to the outspoken thoughts of God in Genesis 2:18, when He said, *"It is not good that man should be alone; I will make him a helper comparable to him."* The Hebrew word used for "good" is "TOWB" which means good/ better/ well/ best/ merry/ prosperity/ precious/ fine/ wealth/ beautiful, favour/ glad.

Incorruptible Beauty

The LORD God looked at Adam, a man who lived in His presence; a man who was financially wealthy (Eden had gold and precious stones according to Genesis 2:11-13); a man who had a paradise home with all the things that were pleasing to his eyes and good for food; a man whom God gave mighty authority and kingship over all species in the waters, the dry land and the air; a man who was endowed to undertake great tasks of naming all cattle, birds and beasts of the field whilst tending the garden of Eden, tasks that could only be completed by one who had great wisdom and understanding. The Lord God had given Adam a kingdom, power, strength and glory but yet with all that He had given him, the Lord God still saw that it wasn't good! Adam still needed a helper to make everything good and better; he still needed a comparable helpmate who causes him to find favour and prosperity beyond who he was and what he had in that season. The LORD God saw that though Adam has all these things, he still needs a wife to help him be the best version of himself; bringing him gladness, wealth and wellbeing in all aspects of his life. Can you see how great a woman is? Can you behold the powerful influence she is to a man's life?

If more men and women understood the powerful position their roles as helper have within marriage, under the leading of their own husbands, their marriages would be very powerful! Surely, if women knew how to walk fully in their role as helper, their influence within their marriages would be unstoppable!

Therefore, God intended women to be married so that they can play the role of helping their husbands. This role is futile outside marriage and becomes a false facade of what God envisioned for wifehood. Perhaps you are reading this and you are already married but you are failing to walk fully in your role as a helper towards your husband but desire to help? Firstly, you are on the right track by desiring to walk fully in your role as wife. God's Spirit and his Word will enable you to be fully built, continually transformed and mentally fashioned to be everything that God created you to be, not just a wife but also a woman of God and a mother! It is by faith in Christ through the empowerment of God's Spirit that you can do all things through Jesus Christ! Eve's ability to fully express and commit to walking as a helper rested on how God created her. Let's look closely into this creation process in the following chapter.

Creation Process of A Woman

Upon the creation process of Eve, the bible says in Genesis 2:21-22 (AMP), "***And the LORD God caused a deep sleep to fall on Adam, and he slept; He took one of his ribs or part of his side and closed up the (place with) flesh. And the rib or part of his side which the LORD God had taken from the man He built up and made into a woman, and He brought her to the man.***"

Lets look deeper into these two scriptures from the Hebrew wording used:

- ⚔ The word "Rib" in Hebrew is "TSETSE" which means "*side, rib*".

- ⚔ The word used for "Taken" in Hebrew is "LAQACH" which is to "*take, get, fetch, lay hold of, receive*".

- ⚔ The word used for "Made" in Hebrew is "BANAH" which means to "*build, rebuild, establish, cause to continue*".

- ⚔ The word used for "Woman" in Hebrew is "ISHSHAH" which means "*woman, wife, female*".

Therefore, to recap on Genesis 2:21-22 with the full use of Hebrew word meanings, it can be concluded that, "…the LORD caused a deep sleep to fall on Adam, and he slept; He **took/ got/ fetched/ laid hold of/ received** the **side/ rib** and closed up the (place with) flesh. And the **side/ rib** which the LORD God had **taken/ got/ fetched/ laid hold of/ received** from man He **built/ rebuilt/ established/ caused to continue** into a **woman/ wife/ female,** and He brought her to the man."

How marvellous to know that the woman of God is built up, established and has a growing capacity which causes her to continue as a three-fold vessel consisting of being a female, woman and wife! How awesome it is to know that God brought this whole (not premature) being as a 3 in 1 vessel to Adam. Indeed, as it was for the first women in Genesis 2:22, God who never changes, still wants the same for the woman in the 21st century. God wants women to be healed, whole, built up and established in Him, before He can introduce them to a man. God is looking to integrate whole individuals as couples for His glory!

Incorruptible Beauty

Dear reader, are you a woman currently seeking after a man to heal you, build you up and establish you emotionally, physically or financially? Are you putting men on a pedestal that only God can operate infallibly on? Unfortunately, due to many factors that stem from social and economic influences, many women are conditioned to expect men to perform at a standard that only God can! Men are fallible human beings and incapable of bringing a woman to a place of total healing, total wholeness and total establishment; only God can do that. It's written in Matthew 11:28-30, *"Come to Me, all you who labor and are heavy laden, and I will give you rest. Take My yoke upon you and learn from Me, for I am gentle and lowly in heart, and you will find rest for your souls. For My yoke is easy and My burden is light."*

Therefore, in Christ, a woman is in a position to receive total liberation! No longer walking with plundered emotions, trying to hide the wounds of her heart and emotions behind erotically suggestive clothing, excessive makeup, drunkenness, cursing language, clubbing and kissing up on every guy who treats her nicely. Daughter of God, are you hiding your wounds hoping the next guy you get will build you up and restore the brokenness?

Only Jesus can heal you and restore you completely when you stop the relationship cycle of running in the arms of men seeking after hope that only God can illuminate in your heart and life. The LORD Jesus is ready to build you up no matter your age, status, race, background, past mistakes, failures or circumstances. God is willing to take you in His arms and mend you, heal you, cleanse you, beautify you and hold you; before He can let you go in the arms of a man; the arms of one of His precious sons'. The question is, will you let Him? Will you surrender all the broken pieces of your heart or life to Him? (See prayer at the end of this chapter)

In addition, it is written in Genesis 2:22 that "…**He (the LORD God) BROUGHT her to the man…**", but it's important to know Who exactly is bringing the woman to the man. In Scriptures the LORD God is Holiness, Righteousness, Peace, Love etc. If one was to name all the things that the LORD God is, we'd fill the whole world with books concerning this matter.

61

Never the less, all through-out scripture the Person of the LORD God is depicted as being the "Word of God." Revelations 19.13 says, "**He was clothed with a robe dipped in blood, and His name is the Word of God."** and John 1:1-3 says "**In the beginning was the Word, and the Word was with God, and the Word was God. He was in the beginning with God. All things were made through Him, and without Him nothing was made that was made.**" Therefore, it is not just the Person of Jesus Christ that brought Eve to the man. It is Jesus the Word of God transfigured in righteousness, holiness, peace, wisdom, discernment and protection etc. All these attributes and characteristics found in Christ held the woman's hand as she walked with God, to be finally presented as whole, prepared and mature to her one and only husband; Adam. There was a co-operation that took place between the LORD God and Eve during the process and season of her going to meet Adam! Some women today are delayed or failing to meet their husbands simply because they are unwilling to co-operate with the LORD God.

They want to do things their own way; they want to get their godly husband based on their own terms; they want to meet their husband based on their own age or calendar schedules; they want to date and court based on their own understanding. It is important to note that no-one can go and do something that God is saying, unless they can hear God and no-one can hear God unless they walk and live in the Spirit; God is Spirit. Moreover, even if you can hear what God is saying, it takes a willing and obedient heart to do what God says. Are you single today and wanting to meet your God given spouse? Ask yourself, are you co-operating with God regarding your love life or are you telling God what to do regarding your love life? There are seasons and gifts that God wants you and I to experience but unfortunately we won't experience some of these until we co-operate with Him.

Many young women desiring marriage and seeking a spouse may end up frustrated saying that God is not speaking. However, the truth is, God always speaks and maybe they just haven't positioned themselves to hear Him *clearly*!

Some are waiting for God to speak to them in a way that they want, for example, there was a time I sought God for answers during prayer regarding a situation but God did not speak, however, when I began to selflessly praise and sing songs to Him, God began to give me the answers I longed for. The bible says in John 10:27, *"My sheep hear My voice, and I know them, and they follow Me"*. Dear reader, are you like a sheep that has wandered off from Christ by being distracted by the things of this world? Is there so much noise in your life that you can no longer hear the still small voice of God's Spirit? It is dangerous to go through life without listening to God. Examine yourself today, are you still near Christ, near enough to hear Him or have you wandered off? In order to receive instruction concerning the things God has for you (not only regarding a future spouse), you have to hear God first and be willing to obey Him, otherwise you will end up going the wrong direction and doing the wrong things.

Accordingly, Genesis 2:22 says "*Then the rib which the LORD God had taken from the man He made into a woman, and He brought her to the man*". The Hebrew word used for 'brought her" is "BOW", which means "*to go in, enter, come, come in*".

This gives insight into the fellowship Eve had with God before He brought her to her man. It also reflects that Adam's location was a place that the woman needed to go into and enter in, in order to meet with Adam. Sometimes a woman can be whole and fully prepared for marriage but the man who is meant to be her husband may not be able to <u>see</u> her even if she is within his eye proximity. This is because perhaps she has not yet arrived to the spiritual, emotional and physical location where her husband can recognise and see her. Perhaps you are a single woman trying to be located by your husband today? Ask yourself, have you surrendered your whole heart to God by allowing Him to get bring you to a place where you can be in the same space in Christ physically, emotionally and spiritually with the spouse He has created for you? Do you trust God with your love life or are you distracted by your age, background and miscellaneous circumstances that have no power over God fulfilling your prayer requests?

Another example is that two people can see each other but not <u>meet</u> each other. For instance, a man's future wife can be located in the same church as her future husband and they can even sit two seat rows apart every Sunday but still not meet in person.

As an illustration, Eve was formed, fashioned and established in that same garden of Eden that Adam was put in but it took God's leading to get Eve to "BOW" (Hebrew word for 'Brought Her' meaning - *to go in, enter, come, come in*) and meet Adam. Child of God, in life it's going to take co-operation and obedience to God's leading in order to meet the person, enter the season or receive the things that God has prepared for you! Are you willing today to start to fully co-operate with God in the areas of your life that you have semi shut or completely shut Him out of? Say "LORD God I am willing, I surrender (enter the area) fully to You; by Your Holy Spirit, teach me obedience to Your voice and directions, in Jesus name, Amen".

Evidently, Eve had a relationship with God before she met Adam. She had a conversation with God first before she could qualify to have one with a man. Nowadays some women are able to talk to their so called "boyfriends" for 2 hours straight on the phone but cannot hold a conversation with God for more than 20 minutes in prayer. How can that be so?

Therefore, it is good for the woman of today to learn from the first woman, how she walked with God first before she could know how to walk hand in hand with a man. How she saw the LORD God taking His steps and walking (this is to symbolise God's needs and wants) first before she saw how Adam took his steps and walked (symbolising a man's needs and wants). Eve met the LORD God first, before she met her Adam. Dear reader, do you have a meeting place with God? A daily devotional time of prayer? Do you have conversations with the Holy Spirit not only when you need something but even just to say "Hi Holy-Spirit my Counsellor who dwells in me, I want to tell You that I love You"? Having a daily relationship with God is not a burdensome task, in-fact it is the most fulfilling life you can ever have on a daily basis! A personal relationship with God exceeds that of the sweetest and greatest boyfriend, girlfriend, wife or husband; in the world.

Therefore, the correct pattern for entering any relationship is allowing Jesus first to have your heart, then He can entrust it to one of his royal son's care. Many a times, out of loneliness, women are running into the arms of a man instead of first running to the embrace of Jesus. A woman who is accustomed to the behaviour of choosing a man first over God, might never come to know what a pure, loyal, beautiful and love filled embrace feels like as she trots up and down the earth looking for a faithful, reliable and worthy man. She will keep on compromising herself and her standards; she will remain mediocre and will keep believing that she's not good enough as the toll of heartbreaks takes over. Is this you? You want a man to complete you but not Christ to complete you? Here's a scenario, the eye view of a woman looking through the window in an aeroplane and eye view of a woman looking through the window in a train are totally different. The eye view of the woman in the train is very limited from she in the aeroplane; so it is with Christ. The more you get to know Jesus Christ by growing in the Word of God, the more your views on men and yourself become excellently greater and unlimited. You just won't be able to compromise yourself any longer because you will know your worth. Perhaps you have been in relationships whereby you were abused and ill-treated? If so, it's time to get healed today by refusing to let Satan intimidate you any longer when he reminds you of your past.

This, Satan will do to rob you of your role of submission in a future marriage or present marriage, that you may be like Jezebel whose name means "un-husbanded one" because she hates submission and uses control to manipulate a man to submit to her.

As a consequence of an unhealed life, some woman tend to resent men by not wanting a man in their lives, opting for a lesbian lifestyle or being a 'toxic source of advise' to other ladies in their lives. If these women are relatives or friends they will say things like, "men are trouble" or "there's no good men!"; this is a lie that stems from bitterness. Dear reader, are you a woman who is becoming bitter and resentful of men based on your past hurts? Once you forgive that man (or men) and forgive yourself too; this will be the beginning of your deliverance and healing. Forgive them today! Forgive yourself today! Receive the healing of Jesus Christ right now into your heart and life as you make the final choice of forgiveness! Say "LORD Jesus Christ, I forgive (insert name) and I receive total healing and power from bitterness and resentment right now in Jesus name, Amen."

Live a life free from compromise and allow the word of God to fill the empty spaces in your heart that were once filled with bitterness and resentment.

Finally, it is written in Genesis 2:22 "...**He brought her to the man...**". Eve didn't go around chasing after Adam! God brought her to him after completing her. Are you looking for a man by chasing after a man? If so, watch out, you might need to continue chasing after him even when he is yours! The enemy can use the thirst of our strongest desires to trap us, this is why we must never become so thirsty for something such that we are willing to take any cup of refreshment that is offered to us; not every cup has clean water. Are you willing to get any Christian "godly" man because of your thirst for marriage? Remember, just because he is a "godly" man, doesn't mean he is your "godly" man! Realise within yourself, without any doubt or fear that the only flawless vehicle to receiving a husband is through Jesus Christ. He is the pointer on the compass. Remember how Eve was hidden in Adam as his rib?

You won't have to look far neither, if you allow God to lead you. With God all things are possible; He can lead you into the arms of your Adam even in the most unlikely places. The most important thing is being led by God! His works are the same yesterday, today and forever; just like He did in the garden of Eden, He will do now and lead you into your future husband's sphere whether it's spiritually, emotionally or physically. However, there's a requirement of maturity needed on your part, that when the time comes to meet your Adam; you are presented whole. Eve needed to be built up into a female, a woman and a wife, before she could be presented as a bride to her groom Adam. There was a need for wholeness on her part because in order for her to play the full role of "helper" she needed to be mature enough to carry the responsibility of a marriage when she met her husband. Although every love story is different, it is always ideal that maturity and wholeness is present before couples say "I do". It takes two godly individuals to make a godly marriage; true godliness comes as a result of one's life being submitted to God's Word. Indeed, a whole man and a whole woman are able to create a whole marriage through Jesus Christ.

Eve was at one point premature, she was just a rib; though she indeed played the role of a rib in Adam's body by protecting the heart of Adam and holding his lungs safely within a closed rigid box; she was still premature for that role outside the body. Are you wanting to be a wife yet you are premature to play the role of wife inside marriage? Eve would have been useless to Adam if God had presented her to him as a rib and not as a "ISHSHAH" that is female, woman and wife. Dear reader, are you crying out to God for a husband but yet you are not yet whole emotionally, financially or spiritually? Are you still like an internal rib? You are still bleeding and unformed for the role of "helper"? Ask yourself, if the husband comes now, will you be of use to him or will it be a case of meeting the right person at the wrong time? What a disaster it is when spouses meet each other at the wrong times! Therefore, daughter of God, it's not the man you need the most, it is God. You need God to be your number one before you make any man your number one. When God is your main concern, then He will give you a man who will share this same love, concern and joy with you.

Dephne Madyara

A Woman's Purpose and Role

In a world that has easy access to genital sex changes and open transgender lifestyles, the description of what a female is, has become complex to pin point. In a society where feminism is becoming very prevalent it can become difficult to define what the role of a woman is; the role of attached to her God-given identity. As we read earlier according to Genesis 2:22 (KJV) which says, ***"And the rib, which the LORD God had taken from man, made he a woman, and brought her unto the man."*** We saw that the Hebrew word used in place of woman is "ISHASH" which not only means woman but also means wife and female.

The role of a woman is attached to her identity of being a woman, wife and female. God fearfully and wonderfully made the woman to a powerful 3 in 1 influence but the enemy tries to fight her identity through disguised forms of distortion. Never the less, God is the same yesterday and today and His Word never changes. It's important that despite the standards of living and demonic influences we see taking place, women must still stand on God's Word in order to be victorious as individuals that

God created them to be, in order to fully walk in their purposes and roles as women, wives and females.

A Woman of God

After a woman accepts the LORD Jesus Christ as her Lord and Saviour, the LORD desires to teach and help her by His Holy Spirit how to be a woman of God for God's glory. Women have a very special place in God's heart; Jesus Christ Himself after His resurrection, revealed Himself first to a woman named Mary Magdalene and commissioned her to speak to the brethren (His disciples) about His ascension to heaven. This one sign and moment of grace drowned many centuries of religion and prejudice towards women (read John 20:1-17). There is a grace that women have but unfortunately some born again women don't make use of this grace by allowing it to mold them into women of God. God made both men and women not just to be Christian men and women but to be men and women of God. Many think that a woman or man of God is a title for individuals who are pastors, prophets or preachers but that is far from the truth!

Dephne Madyara

Being a man or woman of God is not dependant on having a congregation but on walking with God daily and letting Him lead you in His path's of righteousness for His name's sake. It's about being led by His Spirit on a daily basis; living a life surrendered to His Word. For example, the biblical figure Boaz was known for his business exploits and wealth, however, he is an example of man of God based on his character, behaviour and life; throughout the book of Ruth chapters 2 to 4. Hence, a woman can be a woman of God at her work place, her business, university or at home with her family etc.

Today some single women are racing through their season of single-hood chasing after the role of "helper" instead of first discovering the role of a "woman of God". They don't realise that in order to even begin functioning as a helper, they will need to draw from their reservoir of being a "woman of God". For how can a wife serve a husband privately if she cannot serve God privately? Daughter of God, are you too busy trying to be found by a man to the point that you are neglecting your role of being a woman of God towards God, your family and outsiders?

Incorruptible Beauty

Do you know that Jesus Christ is a woman's first love and husband? Jesus is the first love of the Church (see Revelations 2:2-6). God can use you as a woman of God to bring light into this world on a small, average or large scale. It's important for every woman to cultivate herself into a woman of God by growing in the knowledge and love of Christ. This is why the season of single hood is very crucial and needs to be spent in discovering Christ rather than in bitterness from the impatience of tomorrow. What a waste of joy it is, living your today by chasing for tomorrow! Therefore, don't strive to only grow into a woman (an adult female) but strive to grow into a woman of God. There are ideas, gifts, talents, abilities and mysteries that God has hidden in every women and sometimes a woman's selfless praise to God is the key that will bring these things out. Sometimes her daily devotional bible studies will manifest these things more clearly in her life. Sometimes her fervent prayers will protect these things from fading away within her. Sometimes her fasts will strengthen and grow these things as she walks in Christ. Other times her daily obedience to God in small and big things will multiply these things.

Sadly, not every woman is willing to tap into this privilege of grace that every believer has, in order to train and discover how to be a woman of God through the Holy Spirit of God. It's written in 1 Corinthians 2:9-10 *"... eye has not seen, nor ear heard, nor have entered into the heart of man the things which God has prepared for those who love Him", but God has revealed them to us through His Spirit. For the Spirit searches all things, yes, the deep things of God".*

It is no wonder why so many women compete with each other; no wonder why there's so much insecurity in churches amoung women; it is no wonder why there are thousands of copies of the one same woman in ministry, the messages preached and the songs sung are beginning to sound the same. There is little originality and evolution simply because women are not willing to spend time sitting at the feet of Jesus in order to be molded fully to reflect a *unique* facet of the glory of Christ to the world. Very few are willing to endure through when the Holy Spirit's pokes, pulls and plucks them during the process of pruning so that they can reflect an incomparable glory of God through their lives.

Sadly, some women would rather take the easy road and copy what so and so is doing, hope for the best and if fortunate, achieve a quick success. This leaves no room for individuality nor maturing in one's original identity and unfortunately, easy roads never leave any legacy; the names of those who walked on the common path are not often remembered tomorrow. Dear reader, are you hoping that if you did what so and so is doing then you will end up where they are or having what they have? Are you allowing people to tell you to be like someone else in order to achieve a certain status or level of success? There is already a quality of genius within you, why do you need to be like someone else? Discover yourself through the Spirit of God and live out your best self because being in Christ sets you apart from being average, you become empowered by the power of God within and have access to God's Word that is able to transform your mind to conform to Christ's way of thinking. A woman of God will never need to strive to be like someone else because she knows who she is in Christ, that there is only one her and there will never be anyone like her. She does not compete but always tries to outdo her yesterday rather than outdoing other people.

Dear reader, there is only one you and there will never be another you! Allow these words to sink into your spirit.

The biblical figure Mary Magdalene was not perfect, she was in fact the bible says she was a sinner (see Luke 7:37) and used her expensive gifts (perfume) to please others until she met Jesus Christ. Mary Magdalene chose to forsake her old ways and used her expensive gifts on Christ, she chose to sit at the feet of Jesus, giving her whole heart to discovering Him as written in this passage of scripture in Luke 10:38-42, *"Now it happened as they went that He entered a certain village; and a certain woman named Martha welcomed Him into her house. And she had a sister called Mary, who also sat at Jesus' feet and heard His word. But Martha was distracted with much serving, and she approached Him and said, "Lord, do You not care that my sister has left me to serve alone? Therefore tell her to help me." And Jesus answered and said to her, "Martha, Martha, you are worried and troubled about many things. But one thing is needed, and Mary has chosen that good part, which will not be taken away from her.""*

Incorruptible Beauty

Today, Mary Magdalene is not only the first woman but first person (see John 20:1-18) who saw the Lord Jesus Christ when He rose from the dead! Dear reader, will you choose that good part? Choosing Christ will transform your life in ways you cannot imagine. God desires for women to spend enough time with Him so that they can discover who they are as women of God irregardless of their status. It's in God's presence that our minds become aware of our hidden identity in Christ.

Perhaps, are you asking yourself what your gifts are or who you are in Christ? If so, I want you to know that I was once there too 7 years ago. I wanted to know what my place was in the body of Christ, what my gifts and calling was. I wanted to know who I was in Christ so I made a decision to find out who Jesus was because I knew that if I discovered more of Him, I would discover myself in the process. Around 2011-2012 I quit my part-time job and university degree to study the bible for 6 hours a day from Monday to Friday starting from Genesis to Revelations and on Saturdays I would fast and pray. It was very difficult in the first few weeks because this was going against my normal routines and schedules but I was determined to grow so I would use my phone alarm and set calendar diaries so that I don't procrastinate. My social life became non-existent because I could no longer hang out with my cousins and friends as often I wanted. However, I began to be so hungry for the Word that it became my delight. The bible began to be so alive to me, such that the emotional and psychological wounds I had, began to be healed by the Word of God; it's as if the Words would jump inside my heart and be a healing balm as I read them. Do you believe that the Word of God is powerful enough to heal you from brokenness, fear, low self esteem, guilt and heart break? Believe in the power of God's Word! Now, during that time the Lord also told me plainly what my calling was during prayer and in those days I began to have child-like faith that I would have an encounter with the LORD Jesus Christ, so I would sweep and clean my room every night before I sleep, thinking to myself that if He comes at least my bedroom will be presentable for the King of kings. The LORD honoured my faith and He visited me in a vision. In the vision with His hand He put His Words into my heart and anointed me to write and minister His heart to the Body of Christ. The vision was so real such that when I woke up as one of the angels was putting a white transparent-like garment over me, I could still feel the sensation of the garment falling over me. Soon after that night, words began to easily flow from me when I wrote such that I started to exhort people via Christian Facebook groups and then later on started a blog. I didn't understand at that time that the LORD wanted me to write books so the process of writing on Facebook groups and Wordpress blogs was training me to write books. Dear reader, though I'm still on a discovery journey in Christ, however, making the practical decision in 2010 to discover Jesus Christ has helped me to discover my place and unique gifts in the body of Christ. That I'm not only a messenger of Christ but also an author and fashion designer. It's written in Jeremiah 33:2-3, *"Thus says the LORD who made it, the LORD who formed it to establish it (the LORD is His name): 'Call to Me, and I will answer you, and show you great and mighty things, which you do not know.'"*

So then, if you are asking the same questions I asked 7-9 years ago, who you are, what your calling is, what your gifts and talents are, I hope my personal experience can encourage you to discover the LORD Jesus Christ so that you can discover yourself.

Call to Him and He will answer you! It's not to say go and quit your job or education, please don't do that, let those decisions be approved by the Holy Spirit or be led by Him. This is not to say that if you clean your room every night, you will have an encounter with the Lord Jesus Christ, no, but it's to say take a look at your spiritual life; your prayer life; your personal bible study time; your praise outflow; how is that looking? Is it growing, maturing or edifying? It's impossible to spend a lot of time with God and still not grow nor discover yourself in that process. Though the self discovery journey of a believer in Christ is ongoing, the beauty of it is that as the believer discovers Christ more and more, he/she discovers her/himself more clearly. God is looking to raise women of God who can use their God given abilities and gifts to change work places; to edify ministries; to beautify their families, to change countries and the world for God's kingdom. Sadly some are too busy trying to become wives, too busy to seek God, too busy looking at everything they don't have today, too afraid to do what God tells them.

Incorruptible Beauty

A Female

In the days we are living in, a man can wake up and
suddenly identify himself as a woman; at freewill he can
change his male sexual organs to female genitals.
Unfortunately, all of that man's efforts of changing himself
into a woman are futile because God gave the female an
ability that a male cannot and does not have. God made
the male to carry seed (sperm) and gave the female the
ability to incubate and grow that seed. Though there are
some pregnancy and conception issues that can take place
in the female body, God purposed the female body
uniquely from that of a male's and gave it ability to
conceive and give birth after reaching puberty. Indeed,
after puberty a female can bear children and breastfeed;
she has capability to produce offspring. We not only see
the power of fertility in the female human being but also in
plants and animals; all are uniquely identified as either
male or female in that respect. Therefore, no matter how
feminine a transgender or homosexual wants to behave; no
matter if he changes his genitals to a woman's; no matter if
goes through a successful hormone replacement therapy
to feminise himself; the truth of the matter is that a male will
never truly be a female.

Today, scientists are frantically trying to research and invent ways to get men to also have wombs so that they can conceive and give birth, all under the emblem of equality, when in fact, this concept of men having wombs is conspired by Satan the master manipulator and liar! A male was created to be a male and a female to be a female; God does not make mistakes as it is written in Psalm 139:13, ***"For Your formed my inward parts; You covered me in my mother's womb."***

Subsequently, with femininity also comes certain behaviours and attributes that come as a result of being fashioned as a female and these can range from being girly, emotional, very sensitive, compassion, caring etc. It's good for women of God to love the attributes that are attached to them. However, it can be confusing to come to a point where you accept yourself fully and are not be intimidated by the attributes attached to your gender chromosome, when so many voices are telling you what you should be and how you should behave. If you are quite emotional and society is telling you that this is a sign of weakness are you going to bow down to that opinion?

Incorruptible Beauty

If you are naturally bubbly, loud and animated in your tone and behaviour are you going to tone it down because society says you need to be more quieter to be likeable? If you are dimming down your light based on what friends and society expect of you, how many more things about you will you dull down for others on this road of your own life? During my college years before I was a born again Christian, a lot of people tried to box me in; some of my male college mates would say to me "Dephne you are too nice, you're too soft, you need to toughen up a bit because guys may take advantage of you". I didn't understand why I needed to be tougher and louder in order to cocoon myself from danger. Later on after college when I got saved some people in ministry would still say the same thing to me, that I was too nice, too soft spoken or too this and that but the LORD God began to teach me that He made me this way, that I was fearfully and wonderfully made! God eventually blessed me with a man who is more "nicer" than i am according to society. When we were just friends and I had just accepted Jesus Christ as my Lord and Saviour in 2007, this man would pick me up from my parents house every Sunday to take me to church; he would drop everything to help me if I needed help with something; he would sit with me in the library once teaching me about Jesus. His interaction with other believers and strangers demonstrates the love of Christ which helped me to understand that being "too nice" is a necessary nature we must possess in Christ. Dear reader, don't let anyone box you in or dim your light because God will eventually bring like-minded people around you who will get you and understand you.

It's crucial that a woman discovers how God fearfully and wonderfully created her so that she can grow to fully embrace herself before society begins to mold her into a caricature of herself. Once a woman discovers why she is fearfully and wonderfully made, she will no longer seek to conform to society's demands but her desire as a female and woman, will be to conform to God's word. When you discover how you are fearfully and wonderfully made you will learn to grow your strengths; you will learn how to edify your personality, behaviour and character so beautifully and uniquely whilst conforming them to God's Word. Don't change yourself because certain people don't like who you are and how you behave. Style wise, if your style and personality is very girly why change this to fit a category?

If your style and personality is tomboyish why change this to fit in a category? For instance, i wear midi length pencil dresses and heels about 90% of the time; this is my style but some female colleagues at a 9-5 job began to ask me why I was always dressed up. The truth is I wasn't dressing up but I was just being myself. Sometimes what is normal to you regarding your personality, style, attributes, outlook and femininity may not be deemed as normal to others but that is the beauty of individuality (as long as it's not rebellion towards God).

Dear reader, God will bring you people who will support you even in the least relevant of things, friends who will accept all of you without being intimidated; acquaintances that can treasure the things that God has put inside you. Therefore, daughter of God, learn to treasure the feminine things about you, they add to your uniqueness. Don't allow circumstances, environments and hardships to eat away at your femininity and your ability to be feminine in words, actions or behaviour.

A Wife

Often times the title of wife is sort after by many single women but yet, the title itself is like a well with no water because the substance of wifehood comes at a price. A wife of noble character who can find? It will take obedience and submission to God's Word and Spirit in order to be victorious in order to be a daily success as a wife. Women must desire to be filled daily with godly knowledge and power within them prior to becoming wives so that they can demonstrate that fullness within the sphere of marriage. Genesis 2:23 says "This *is* now bone of my bones and flesh of my flesh; she shall be called Woman, because she was taken out of Man." When Adam exclaimed these revelational words to his wife, this affirmation were not only confirming his wedding vows to her but also revealing their marital roles and identities. That Eve was the ultimate helper to Adam and he, her ultimate covering as head. Sometimes women get married but they can take years to finally come to a place where they see their husband as head over every area of their lives. A wife must know and recognise her covering.

It's so crucial on the day that they marry that she understands and recognises her husband's place in her life not only financially but more so spiritually, physically, sexually and emotionally. From the day she says "I do" to him, she must begin to recognise him as her covering.

There was peace and harmony in Eden until Eve stopped recognising Adam as her head and she became tempted; lust began to grow in the eyes of Eve, leading her to a place of rebellion. Sometimes there is no peace in marriages simply because the wife does not see her husband as her head; her limited perception spills over to her thoughts, meditations of the heart and alternatively her actions of disrespect. Even if he has lost his job, he is still the head; even if he is not as spiritually mature as his wife, he is still the head; mature helpers help (not offend) their husbands to walk as their heads but immature helpers shove their husbands into walking as the head. In marriage Satan will try very hard to blind wives from looking at the their husbands as their covering. Satan knows that wives are homemakers and uses this to gain a foothold into their home. He knows that if she can't see her husband as her covering sexually, he can steal their joy in the marriage bed.

Satan knows that if she can't see her husband as her covering emotionally, he can steal her ability to submit physically which in turn provokes the husband to cave in. Submission allows the husband to securely stand in and walk in his role of covering his wife.

Today, we are hearing endless stories of pastors taking advantage of women in their congregations by using their position of authority to entice or control them. For example, a male pastor counselling another man's wife alone and telling her not to tell her husband what was discussed in that session! Why is this happening? If women were to fill themselves with the knowledge of God's Word they would discern what is proper and what is improper during their counselling sessions. They would know that marriage means being one; that marriage demands complete transparency; that everything discussed with the pastor must be disclosed to their husbands at home because they are one by covenant and no pastor, prophet, deacon or bishop must separate their oneness!

Moreover, in churches it is possible to see a wife giving her pastor more respect than she ever shows her own husband at home. Such things ought not to be so. The bible says in 1 Corinthians 11:3, *"but I want you to know that the head of every man is Christ, the head of woman is man, and the head of Christ is God."* Due to 21st century doctrinal error, wives may become swayed to submit to their pastors more than they do their own husbands, yet, it is God who created marriage and perfects it! Now although church leaders are to be obeyed and be submitted to by the congregation according to Hebrews 13:17, it is however crucial to understand that the spiritual covering of the congregation and the individuals in the congregation, is not the church leader but it is the LORD Jesus Christ (see Colossians 1:18). This is why the LORD can tell an individual to leave a church and become a pastor but that individual's pastor might not understand this unless the Holy Spirit reveals it to them, for God is the only Spiritual Father. He is the Supreme One and it is He who holds the breath of life of every human being in His hand. It is written in Matthew 23:9 (AMP), *"Do not call anyone on earth [who guides you spiritually] your father; for One is your Father, He who is in heaven."*

Therefore, it's important that a wife understands that her covering is not her pastor, it's her husband and her husband's covering is Jesus Christ but their spiritual covering is God. So then, when a wife recognises her covering she begins to correctly walk as a helper according to this truth in Ephesians 5:33 (AMP), *"…and the wife [must see to it] that she respects and delights in her husband [that she notices him and prefers him and treats him with loving concern, treasuring him, honouring him, and holding him dear]."*

Indeed, a helper is called to respect her husband in all seasons, respect doesn't mean that they will be no disagreements but that she can in wisdom respectfully disagree; she is called to delight in him sexually, physically and emotionally; to notice him above all men, above her children and above her relatives; to prefer him above all men, above her children and above her relatives; to treat him with loving concern all the days of her life being concerned about his health and doesn't feed him with ready made meals and junk foods but she cooks/prepares nutritional foods; to treasure him even in difficult seasons; to honour him everyday; to hold him dear emotionally, prayerfully and sexually.

Incorruptible Beauty

The role of a helper can only be walked in such a way by a woman who is led and empowered by the Spirit of God; indeed, a woman who submits to the Word of God and delights in it; a woman who is not only wise in spiritual things but also physical things.

Therefore, it's important to understand that being a helper and being a woman of God are two very different things, however, within marriage, both roles work together like two sides of a coin; your strength as a helper lies in your strength as a woman of God. However, many wives have allowed their gifts, callings and talents to lie doormat under the guise of being a helper. It's saddening when their husbands contribute to this loss by not allowing their wives to be all that God created them to be. There are books, fashion houses, property developments, music albums, sermon teachings, national businesses, television programs, jobs etc that are unspoken for and dead because wives are neglecting their purpose in being a woman of God. Are you a wife today but neglecting to start that bachelor's degree you desired to do before you wedded?

Perhaps God has anointed you to be a preacher of His Word but you are neglecting the gift because of prejudice opinions? Are you saying you are too busy as a wife to shine in your entrepreneur gifts? Regrettably, you will find that you won't have peace until you start walking in your calling and gifts! Remember, not matter how old you are or how fast the world is changing today, it's never too late to start walking in your gifts and calling today. God has graced you to be you, step out in faith and walk in your purpose and role as you reflect Christ.

Evaluation

To conclude, you can now see that women were given a womb which signifies the great ability to bear children. You also see that God took the rib from Adam and made it into a woman first before bringing her to her man. She was not premature, she was more than a female and more than a woman, she was built up and moulded into a wife. God had to prepare her as a woman of God for the wifehood calling of "helper". God built her up spiritually, emotionally and physically, so that she can be correctly aligned to this man with a God given vision and calling; evidently women were made to be influential. No wonder the devil is using women to entice men through provocative clothing and outward beauty. Being influential is a great asset if used correctly through humility. One dictatorial husband said to his wife, "I am the head of this house" and the woman responded, "Oh Yeah! You may be the head of this house, but don't forget, I am the neck that turns it around", talk about feminine power and influence! Daughters of God, Satan wants to gain the upper hand on women's lives that he may plug into them his polluted wisdom, to pervert their virtues and birth forth sin and evil.

This is depicted by Jezebel who's influence was only evil and filled with selfishness (see 1 Kings 21:1-16).

The enemy is whispering lies to so many females and convincing them that they are nothing without a sugar daddy, without taking off their clothes for money and that nobody will fall in love with them if they don't wear provocative clothing or excessive make-up. The enemy doesn't want God's daughters to have a relationship with YHWH Jaire (God your Provider) because he knows that when you have a real relationship with God, you will discover that God is your provider, your peace, your shield, your beauty, your healer and best friend. Dear reader, I don't know what lies the devil has been whispering in your ears for many years. Maybe you didn't have a great father or mother, maybe you are a single mother, are you pregnant and considering abortion? Are you feeling hopeless? Has Satan been feeding you with lies, telling you that you are a mistake? Perhaps the enemy has be telling you that you will accomplish nothing in life because of your background and circumstances?

I want you to know that the devil is a liar and has always been lying from the beginning. Nobody born or conceived is a mistake, regardless of how painful and unfair the foundation (e.g. rape) of one's conception came to being, God will still form that child in the womb, as it's written in Psalm 139:16 (GWT), *"**Your eyes saw me when I was only a foetus. Every day [of my life] was recorded in Your book before one of them had taken place**."* This is why abortion is wrong. Do you know that the moment the sperm fertilises the egg, a baby's genetic make-up is complete, including its sex. When a Y sperm fertilizes the egg the baby will be a boy; if an X sperm fertilizes the egg the baby will be a girl. How powerful is that? God sees the conception and begins to plan out its future before the baby is even born. No matter how you got here, God knew you before the foundations of the earth and loved you even when you were a foetus. God wrote all the days of your life when you were in the womb, He planned your steps and footprints and has a plan for you. Are you willing to accept God's plans for you and put yours aside? God's plans are always better than our own. Are you willing to make a decision today to start the journey of discovering Christ's love for you?

As long as you love God, He makes all things that seem to be against you, to work out for your good as it is written in Romans 8:28, "**and we know that all things work out together for good for those who love the LORD and are called according to His purposes**".

Do you know God's plan for your life? His plan and purposes for you are not the same as those for the next woman because God didn't make copies but made each person unique and original. For this reason, He has given you His Holy Spirit who now dwells in you (if you are born again). The Holy Spirit is your Teacher and Helper who will show you all truth concerning God's plan and role for you. You will find this plan in His Scriptures, that's right, you will find it in the bible. It's in the Word of God that you will see who you are and what your gifts and talents are. The Word of God is like a mirror revealing what you look like, it is a make-over transforming wounds, scars and blemishes, making you excellently beautiful; filling you with wisdom and strength. When the Power of the Holy Spirit overshadows you, your life will never be the same again.

Incorruptible Beauty

It's time to indulge and saturate yourself in God's Word remembering always each time you open your bible, to ask the Holy Spirit to teach you and show you the secrets hidden in the Word of God, Amen.

Furthermore, I want to address an issue that is causing stagnation and hindrances from total healing for many women; whether single, dating or in a relationship leading towards marriage. Sometimes the material possessions you are keeping that came from an ex whether as small as a necklace or a valentine card can affect your now relationship "status" or future "status". In marriage, these things actually serve as symbols of idolatry, in the sense of being physical objects of worship to this ex. These gifts can distract and disturb your communion, fellowship and unity between you and the man you are with, in this present relationship whether it's heading towards marriage or not; or the future man you are meant to be with. What you keep can serve as a justification of fellowshipping with the past by saying these gifts from your ex are a part of you and in-sync with your life's traits, plans, purposes and vision. The presence of those things in your life speaks on your behalf saying "you are not going into a marriage "whole" as long as I am present in your life". What this means is when you enter marriage these things will play the part of restricting the full blessing and fruits of a marriage.

Moreover they also restrict the peace, joy, love and fellowship in your present relationship. The world and media teach that if an ex wrongs you or leaves you, at least you can keep the diamonds, shoes and clothes, but in the spiritual and emotional realm this so called "cleverness" is far from being clever. You may suffer loss in strength, endurance, patience, kindness, peace and joy in your present or future relationship because you are keeping and moving around with baggage. You may have deleted your ex's phone number and cut off all communication but why do you still keep the things they gave you? How will you have fellowship with your future when you are still in fellowship with your past? Pause for some minutes to ponder on this, if possible in prayer concerning these things and use godly wisdom, being led by the Holy Spirit as you consider this.

I will give you my testimony but before I do, may you please understand that this may not apply to you or the

Holy Spirit may not ask you to do the same things as He asked me to do, as this is not doctrine but rather my own experience through the grace of God. When I entered courtship, I was naïve and ignorant. I didn't know why I still had emotional wounds despite my efforts of faithful and fervent praying and fasting for healing. Then one day the Holy Spirit said to me "I want you to cut all ties with your ex's, delete all communication lines from your phones, throw away (do not give away) all the shoes and clothes they bought you, burn the diaries you have been keeping." I tell you, I was indignant! However, I gradually and finally obeyed and I praise God till this day! A surgical operation took place in my emotions, mentality and soul when I burnt those diaries, when I binned those shoes and clothes, while declaring the Scriptures. I tell you God was delivering me from the wounds and cracks in my heart, mind and soul that I didn't realise I had. As a matter of fact, some of the wounds healed instantly. I was no longer insecure, jealous, fearful and unrealistic. God healed me because I was ready to take responsibility and was finally transparent, giving Him all the broken pieces of my heart. Sister, sometimes you will get a good man when you are ready to take responsibility for one.

Sometimes, you will enjoy the fruits of a good relationship when you are ready to take responsibility for them. Sometimes, you will be ready to move on from the past when you stop looking and facing back. If this speaks to you, LET IT GO TODAY! Your deliverance is waiting on you, not on God, God has already done His part, it's up to you to go up and take the offer. Let the past go, let all of it go now! Lets pray!

Prayer

Before you ask God to change you, you have to be willing and obedient to change. Its a one off decision that wont take fasting or weeping. Before you ask God to change you, you have to be willing and obedient to God's way of changing you. Praying for change is actually a one off decision you need to make and it won't take fasting or weeping to make. Just decide in your heart that you are willing to now let Jesus Christ be the Master and LORD of your life, looking daily into His mirror which is His Word that you may really begin to see what you really look like and how beautiful you are. It is living (abiding) in His Word that is going to transform you; allowing the Holy Spirit of God to comfort and teach you about God's kingdom and His righteousness. Will you give Him all your heart today, all of the broken pieces? His arms are already open for His daughters, no matter how scarred, broken, bleeding, damaged or unholy they are. Jesus is the Master of healing and beautifying. I want you to know that you are forgiven and by faith. You don't have to feel forgiven to be forgiven.

Just pray this prayer, "Jesus, I'm ready to make you the LORD of my life. Forgive me for not making You the

LORD of my life by putting other men and things before You. Heal me, beautify me and restore me today. Remove the barriers and chains that were limiting me LORD Jesus from discovering You, by Your precious Blood and Holy Spirit Power, teach me Your ways each time I read Your Word, that my ways may be perfect and whole. Thank you Jesus and I love you. Amen."

Practical Prayer Steps

Now plan a schedule for daily bible studying as led by the Spirit. Personally, my daily bible study schedule consists of choosing a book in the bible that I want to study based on what I'm going through in that season of my life and I read one chapter when I wake up in the morning and read the same chapter before I go to sleep. This gives me room to meditate on the chapter through out the day so that if I have any questions or revelations about it, I'm able to get more clarity when I read the chapter again at night before I sleep. Sometimes, the Holy Spirit will speak to me concerning other bible chapters or verses which I then read or look at additionally to my normal schedule.

For example, if the Holy Spirit tells me to read about the fruits of the Spirit in Galatians chapter 5 but yet I'm currently scheduled to be reading the book of Esther; I will go and read about the fruits of the Spirit but I will also continue with my chapter a day schedule and read a chapter in the book of Esther before I sleep.

If you are a fairly new born again Christian, I suggest you read from the book of John, then Matthew throughout to Revelations. Also, be sensitive to the voice of the Holy Spirit if He wants you to look at something else or wants you to spend more time studying, be ready to listen.

Dephne Madyara

Chapter Three

TYPES OF LOVE

Love is the most sought after need on the earth. It is one of the most talked about subjects on the earth. There's different translations and meanings of it all across the world, through different cultures, races, species and behaviours. Many have died for it, others were hated for it, still others were praised for it. If we were to trace its beginning we would not know what date stamp to put on it as it seems excellent enough to be eternal. By the end of this chapter you should be able to weigh the different types of love, the endurance of your own and discern the kind of love you currently have in your own life; to see what type of love you yourself have been walking in. By the end of this chapter you will be able to discern true love from artificial love.

Introduction

In order to know the true meaning of Love it is always important to weigh things with the flawless Word of God, as to look at it from God's perspective. The bible is originally written in Greek and Hebrew before it was translated into English. The word Love has four meanings in the Greek language but in the English language these are translated as Love. Three of those meanings for the word Love are recorded in the Bible as Phileō, Storgos and Agapaō and one is not but however its character is depicted in the book of Song of Solomon as Eros.

Phileō– friendly love

Phileō is brotherly love of brothers and sisters whether they are Christians, real family or not. Phileō means to cherish, to be fond of, to take pleasure in and to affectionately care for. John 21:15-17 (AMP) says, "*When they had eaten, Jesus said to Simon Peter, Simon, son of John, do you love Me more than these [others do – with reasoning, intentional, spiritual devotion, as one loves the Father]? He said to Him, Yes, LORD, You know that I love You [that I have deep, instinctive, personal affection for You, as for a close friend]. He said to him, feed My lambs. Again He said to him the second time, Simon, son of John, do you love Me [with reasoning, intentional, spiritual devotion, as one loves the Father]? He said to Him, Yes, LORD, You know that I love You [that I have a deep, instinctive, personal affection for You, as for a close friend]. He said to him, shepherd (tend) My sheep. He said to him the third time, Simon, son of John, do you love Me [with a deep, instinctive, personal affection for Me, as for a close friend]? Peter was grieved (was saddened and hurt) that He should ask him the third time, do you love Me? And he said to Him, LORD, You know everything; You know that I love You [that I have a deep, instinctive, personal affection for You, as for a close friend]. Jesus said to him, feed My sheep."*

In this passage of Scripture the Greek word the LORD Jesus used for "love" was "AGAPAO" whilst Peter's use of love was "PHILEO". Can you see that the LORD Jesus and Peter were speaking of two different kinds of love? Phileō love is when one has a special interest in another in all purity without any ulterior motive but in sincerity of heart and mind.

This love is exhorted in the bible, that Christians should cherish each other with this love as brethren. This sort of love has qualities of being innocent, natural and genuine as between siblings. It is affectionate and warm.

Although Phileō shows excellent qualities of goodness and kindness, it however has its flaws. Phileō love tends to be very sentimental, emotional and somewhat conditional. It is closely aligned with feelings rather than decisions and tends to be conformed on the conditions of similarities and interests. It is good in friendships but still lacks endurance in the long run because it is not sacrificial. It is this sort of love that many young people call love. They make this decision purely based on how they feel, their similarities and personalities. Love then becomes a word that they quickly fall into it and but once they fall out of it, it becomes difficult to keep those 3 special words "I love you". Phileō is limited as compared to Agapaō when it comes to relationships because it simply will not endure all things. However as children of God we must become trained to have a Phileō attitude by being properly equipped and refined in God's word in order to function in Phileō's strength, that we may honour the command of loving the brethren in Christ.

PHILADELPHIA – brotherly love

Romans 12:10 says "***Be kindly affectionate to one another with brotherly love, in honour giving preference to one another.***" The Greek word used for "*love*" is "*PHILADELPHIA*". Philadelphia is like brotherly love and family love; it is a love based on kindness, of cherishing one's kindred, especially parents or children and reciprocal tenderness of parents and children. It is similar to Phileo and is a requirement in the Christian faith towards other Christians. It is a caring love whereby you feel compassion for one another. It is a natural love that has been placed in every human being, and is easily expressible. However, this love can be manipulated or flawed in the sense of being based on conditions of upbringing and specific environments. For example, some may not know how to express compassionate care because they didn't grow up being shown this kind of care. Others may have been physically or emotionally abused in their early childhoods and were not fortunate enough to have experienced this kind of love.

Moreover, unfortunately Philadelphia tends to function well in familiar territories and when it is taken out of its familiar territory, ideas, places or people; it then becomes somewhat dysfunctional, but thanks be to God who has given us all His Holy Spirit! It's written in John 14:26 (AMP), *"But the Helper (Comforter, Advocate, Intercessor, Counselor, Strengthener, Standby), the Holy Spirit, whom the Father will send in My name [in My place, to represent Me and act on My behalf], He will teach you all things. And He will help you remember everything that I have told you."* Therefore, the Holy Spirit is able to counsel those who don't know how to be kindly affectionate towards their children or spouses due to their upbringing. Indeed the Holy Spirit is able to strengthen those who don't know how to give preference to their kindred and family. Perhaps you are one of those who doesn't know how to be affectionate, maybe you want to be but are afraid or feel uncomfortable? Just say " Holy Spirit my Helper, empower me today to walk fully in Philadelphia love towards my spouse, my children, my family, (insert if necessary). Teach me the beauty of family love as you empower me in this new territory of walking in family love. Thank You Holy Spirit. Amen"

AGAPAO – unconditional love

1 John 4:16 says, "**And we have known and believed the love that God has for us. God is love, and he who abides in love abides in God, and God in him.**" The words used for love in this Scripture is written in Greek as "AGAPAO". This is Christ-like love which is selfless, sacrificial and unconditional. It totally gives up its own interests, needs and wants for the sake of the other. For example, a Christian who walks in the Agapaō kind of love is able to love a homosexual or prostitute (the sinner) but hate homosexuality and prostitution (the sin). This is the highest and greatest type of love. This sort of Love is impossible to express through our imperfect human nature, but only through the Spirit of God is it attainably possible to express. Hence, it is written in Romans 5:5, "**...the Love of God has been poured out in our hearts by the Holy Spirit who was given to us**". This is because the human nature is fallible, but only God is infallible and able to do all things without flaw. This love is already available in full measure in the hearts of all who believe in Jesus Christ and they need not ask for it.

Therefore by the counsel, wisdom, direction, comfort, strength, leading and help of the Holy Spirit of God in you, you will be able to express Agapaō Love. When you faithfully and perpetually let the Holy Spirit be your Leader, this enables Him to express His love fully through you without hinderance. This type of love is mandatory in marriage and without it, a marriage will be unhappy and limited. It is also the love that God calls all believers to walk in daily. The character of Agapaō's love is described perfectly in 1 Corinthians 13:4-8 and the explanations are as follows:-

Suffers Long - in Greek "makrothymeō meaning that it doesn't lose heart. This love preservers bravely even in troubles. It is slow to anger or to be pained because it can bear long in offences. It is self restraint.

Kind - in Greek "chrēteuomai" meaning kindness. This love gives of self in all purity and not to gain back. It is selfless.

Does Not Envy - in Greek "zēoōou" to mean that it cannot be zealous in pursuit of other's possessions. This love cannot earnestly strive for the things of another through covetousness.

Does Not Parade Itself - in Greek "perpereuomai ou" meaning to boast of one's self. Agapaō cannot display itself through its own extolling. This love has the face of humility and is always willing to serve others because it cannot flaunt itself.

Not Puffed Up - in Greek "ou physioō meaning proud. This love is not swelled up through bearing its own accomplishments and charitable deeds as the world behaves. The world wants to be seen doing charitable deeds in order to get praise but it is not so with Agapaō it cannot be inflated with pride.

Does Not Behave Rudely - in Greek "aschēoneō meaning to act unbecomingly or unseemingly. Agapaō is self controlled and considerate; it cannot act in ignorance.

Does Not Seek its Own - in Greek "zēeōou heautou" meaning to crave or require for oneself. Unlike Eros, Agapaō cannot aim nor strive to please oneself whether by thought, meditation or action.

Is Not Provoked - in Greek "ou paroxynō meaning it cannot be irritated in the sense of altering its measure. This love is so excellent such that anger and scorn cannot change or manipulate it, to make it any lesser than it is.

This is why when those who are in relationships or marriage don't build a foundation of Agapaō they struggle in the times of anger and scorn.

Thinks No Evil - in Greek "logizomai ou kakos" to mean counting and calculating wrongs. This is the facet of Agapaō that is drenched in forgiveness. Agapaō cannot number, inwardly gather and count up every troublesome and destructive action thrown at it. It forgives easily because it is not easily irritated.

Does Not Rejoice In Iniquity - in Greek "chairōou epiadikia" meaning it cannot thrive in injustice whether in the heart or through actions. This love cannot be well in or be glad of unrighteusness. This is what distinguishes love and lust. Infatuation and lust thrive for a season in sin but Agapaō cannot abide in sin because it is pure love.

Rejoices In The Truth - in Greek "sygchairōalēheia" meaning it takes part in rejoicing in all things that are of truth. This love does not spectate about the truth but it celebrates truth and despises falsehood.

Bears All Things - in Greek "stegōpas" meaning to cover or thatch all types of things. Agapaō protects and preserves all things. It is so bearing that it conceals the faults and errors of others so as to protect them from exposure. For example, Jesus knew that Judas was not only a thief but that he would betray Him but never did Jesus call him out for it to expose him but concealed the matter such that none of the disciples knew what Judas was going to do, Jesus protected Judas weakness from all the other disciples. Agapaō love protects, even its enemies.

Believes All Things - in Greek "pisteuōpas" meaning it places confidence in all things by being positive in all circumstances because it has no fear and has nothing to lose or gain. Agapaō is persuaded in all its fullness of Love towards everyone and everything.

Hopes All Things - in Greek "elpizōpas" meaning it hopes with full confidence in all things in terms of the things of God. Through hope it trusts with joy.

Endures All Things - in Greek "hypomenōpas" meaning it remains and perseveres in all situations and towards all people. Agapaō bears calmly and bravely even in ill treatments, misfortunes and trials.

Never Fails - in Greek the word used for never is "oudepote" and the word for fails is *"ekpiptōi "* meaning that

Agapaō never or at any time falls out/down from its position by being powerless or without effect, no matter the situation. Agapaō does not fail.

EROS – erotic love

Eros love is romantic or sexual desire, designed to be physically expressed between a husband and his wife. Although this love is very exhilarating, it is however the weakest of all the four types of Love. It tends to be unreliable because it is built on attraction and desire. This kind of love has a need to be fulfilled, hence, making it somewhat self centred. Its survival is purely based on situations, outlooks and circumstances and is incapable of persevering when these change because it thrives when everything is rosy and perfect but when the storms, the heat of arguments and hurtful disagreements come, it immediately shrivels up like a withered flower and dies.

For these reasons, many relationships are failing because they are built on the foundation of Eros Love, in the sense that they entered the relationship purely based on sexual desire and physical attractions.

It is a sign of immaturity and folly when a relationship is built on Eros; this depicts the content of being naive in the hearts of those involved. Never the less, God created this love, and that it be expressed between a man and his wife as their bodies now belong to each other and not to themselves. He created it to be good, beautiful and ironically enough – to be pure. For it to continually celebrate and aid the process of becoming one between the husband and his wife. Eros only becomes tarnished and seared when it is partaken of outside God's will, for example, fornication, adultery, sodomy, lesbianism etc. The standard and character of Eros Love is proved and depicted in the bible in the book of Song of Solomon. Nowadays, this love has become poisoned and diluted such that if I were to ask you what you think of erotic love, it may be hard for you to picture its innocence, privacy and sacredness between a man and his wife. Rather it's easier to see a picture of pornography, orgies, one night stands, drunken sex, promiscuity and every immoral thing. This ought not to be so!

Despite these criticisms, human beings were given emotions and hormones to have feelings of sexual desire. Therefore, when one feels these sort of desires, this is completely natural as it is in the human nature because our bodies were created to feel this way. Due to our hormones, senses and mind; our bodies will naturally crave to be loved and appreciated as we enter the adolescent stages. However, wisdom is justified by its actions and likewise foolishness is justified by its actions. It is what you do with those feelings and desires that is crucially significant; it's what you do about the desires you are feeling, the sexual thoughts you are having because Eros is to be expressed fully within the context of marriage only. If you are allowing these desires and feelings to make you fornicate or commit adultery; that is sin. Dear reader, are you using these feelings to act on them by watching pornography, masturbating or lusting after the opposite sex? These acts are all forms of bondage that need to be constantly fed and can cause serious problems in a marriage or before marriage if not dealt with. 1 Corinthians 7:9 (AMP) says, "***However, if you cannot control your desires, you should get married. It is better for you to marry than to burn [with sexual desire].***" This passage of scripture was to show that it is not a sin to feel these desires but it is a sin to manifest them in a wrong context that does not conform to God's will.

Are you having strong desires and you are afraid that you can't control them? Perhaps you are in a relationship but you want to honour God and not fall into temptation? Your biggest weapon to overcoming this is filling your mind with the Word of God, it's written in 2 Corinthians 10:5 (NLV) "***We break down every thought and proud thing that puts itself up against the wisdom of God. We take hold of every thought and make it obey Christ***". Take hold of your thoughts, you have power to set your mind and heart on Christ the Author and Perfecter of your faith. Each time you are overcome by these desires just say, " Holy Spirit help me to honour God in my way of thinking, Amen."

Chapter Four

RELATIONSHIPS

When you are asked about what a relationship is what do you think of? Trust, Loyalty, Commitment, Sex, Kissing, Cuddling? In you are single, dating, courting or engaged, in this chapter you will learn the flaws and strengths of a relationship. You will begin to understand the plan of God for a man and a woman in a relationship. By the end of this chapter you will have wisdom on the three dimensions of a relationship, to discern the important steps and principles to take towards the road to marriage whether you are dating or courting. You will be able to weigh the character and vision of your relationship or future relationship, understanding God's earthly and spiritual plan for relationships so that you may walk in God's wisdom in your love life.

Introduction

Some enter relationships because they are looking for a mother or father to do everything for them in their relationships; some go in relationships to gratify their sexual needs; others go in relationships to fill the void of loneliness; still others go in relationships to gain and enjoy material gifts and experiences i.e. shopping trips, dining or traveling. Dear reader if you are currently in a relationship, what was the motive for you to enter it? God takes relationships very seriously and He desires them to be holy and pure, to be founded on selfless love like Christ who died for the church; this is the standard God sets for those who wish to marry, to follow. True love in relationships is built on good soil (heart) immaculately founded on commitment, communication and trust; among other important things. Hence, it's important to define what a relationship is through God's word because unfortunately according to God's Kingdom and principles there are some relationships that are not defined, for example, there is nothing like boyfriend and girlfriend biblically.

Therefore, in order to define a relationship we will look at the 3 types of environments for every type of relationship according to God's standards to identify and define the authenticity of pre-marital relationships.

God's Standard for Relationships

1 Corinthians 13:1-8 says "*Though I speak with the tongues of men and of angels, but have not love, I have become sounding brass or a clanging cymbal. And though I have the gift of prophecy, and understand all mysteries and all knowledge, and though I have all faith, so that I could remove mountains, but have not love, I am nothing. And though I bestow all my goods to feed the poor, and though I give my body to be burned, but have not love, it profits me nothing. Love suffers long and is kind; love does not envy; love does not parade itself, is not puffed up; does not behave rudely, does not seek its own, is not provoked, thinks no evil; does not rejoice in iniquity, but rejoices in the truth; bears all things, believes all things, hopes all things, endures all things. Love never fails. But whether there*

are prophecies, they will fail; whether there are tongues, they will cease; whether there is knowledge, it will vanish away."

The Greek word used for Love throughout this passage of Scripture is "AGAPAO". As you learnt in the previous chapter, Agapaō is the highest kind of love due to it being unconditional. This is the love God expects us to walk in because He demonstrated it through the life of Jesus Christ the Son of God, who even unto death on the Cross demonstrated Agapaō. Moreover by His Holy Spirit, this love is poured out fully in our hearts, so that we too can demonstrate it through the example of Christ our LORD. This kind of love has no middle ground or corners. Hence, there are 3 relationship environments of which Love functions in all its perfection and purity according to God's WORD and these are:-

- ⚜ Love towards God – Matthew 22:37 says, "*Jesus said to him, "You shall love the LORD your God with all your heart, with all your soul, and with all your mind.*""

- ⚜ Love in marriage between a husband and wife – Ephesians 5:22-33 says, "*Wives, submit to your own husbands, as to the LORD. For the husband is head of the wife, as also Christ is head of the church; and He is the Saviour of the body. Therefore, just as the church is subject to Christ, so let the wives be to their own husbands in everything. Husbands, love your wives, just as Christ also loved the church and gave Himself for her, that He might sanctify and cleanse her with the washing of water by the word, that He might present her to Himself a glorious church, not having spot or wrinkle or any such thing, but that she should be holy and without blemish. So husbands ought to love their own wives as their own bodies; he who loves his wife loves himself. For no one ever hated his own flesh, but nourishes and cherishes it, just as the LORD does the church. For we are members of His body, of His flesh and of His bones. "For this reason a man shall leave his father and mother and be joined to his wife, and the two shall become one flesh." This is a great mystery, but I speak concerning Christ and the church. Nevertheless let each one of you in particular so love his own wife as himself, and let the wife see that she respects her husband.*"

- ⚔ Love towards your neighbour – Matthew 22:39 (AMP) says, "The second is like it, 'You shall love your neighbor as yourself [that is, unselfishly seek the best or higher good for others].'"

When Love is incorrectly expressed outside these 3 categories it becomes somewhat volatile and distorted, for example, according to the world's standards it's normal to express the marriage love between husband and wife to a neighbour, which according to society's words that neighbour is a "girlfriend" or "boyfriend". So then, the boyfriend and girlfriend kiss, touch and have sex like a husband and wife are entitled to. However, in the eyes of God that type of relationship is tainted, for how can one express to their brother/sister in Christ or their neighbour, the kind of love between a husband and wife? As a result, some boyfriends and girlfriends are playing husband and wife and enemy sees their error and uses this to torment them and their relationships. Through lack of wisdom, such a couple might not realise that they are actually taking advantage and abusing the love that falls in the category of "Love towards your neighbour". The bible says in 1 Thessalonians 4: 3-6, ***"For this is the will of God, your sanctification: that you should abstain from sexual immorality; that each of you should know how to possess his own vessel in sanctification and honor, not in passion of lust, like the Gentiles who do not know God; that no one should take advantage of and defraud his brother in this matter, because the Lord is the avenger of all such, as we also forewarned you and testified."***

For how can one touch and kiss their neighbour who is meant to be like a brother or sister in the Lord, like how a husband or wife would do to each other? Are they not much rather meant to respect them like they would a sister or brother? Is it not immoral and unethical to touch, kiss and have sex one's own brother or sister? Though this point may be argued that the person they are touching and kissing is not a blood sister or brother but the reality is, until they walk down the aisle at their wedding, having been officially acknowledged before heaven through their vows; technically he or she is still a brother or a sister and in the eyes of God they are defrauding each other.

Hence, because this love is false it will not triumph over problems and trials. This false love is clearly seen mostly in the youths of today; they are jumping from relationship to relationship, week after week, month after month. Today she is with Harry, next month she is with Andrew and vice versa for the man. It's an ugly cycle that doesn't end until they stop abusing the love that God entrusted them with when He said "you shall love your neighbour as yourself"; until they stop playing husband and wife to a neighbour. This is why when people decide to go in a relationship they must have a perspective of marriage. They must have a vision of where they are going, planning and discussing what and what not to do prior to marriage; this is called wisdom - how to, when to and what to do. Otherwise, they are just wasting their time and risking potential heart wounds which eventually harden the heart if not healed, by making it colder and colder through each heartbreak until it is finally hardened. Dear reader, are you in this dilemma? You are dating and entering relationships for the sake of it with no vision? You might be wondering so how can I get to know the opposite sex without dating or entering a relationship? Let's look at that question next.

Entering a Relationship

The most common mistake made when entering a relationship is entering without a vision of where it is going. This is what is called "dating". You somehow hope for the best because you both haven't agreed on a plan and you have no joint vision. In life everything we do must have purpose and vision in order for that thing to reach the point of accomplishment. You can't accomplish that which you didn't plan for. You cannot have something that you never saw or envisioned. Going into a relationship without a plan or vision is dangerous and is a sign of mediocrity.

Below are the principles of commitment leading to marriage according to biblical standards versus those of worldly standards. The parts where it says optional indicates that this stage can be skipped, depending on the couple's interests:

Stages	World's Standard	God's Standard
1	Friendship (optional)	Friendship
2	Dating	Courtship
3	Engagement (optional)	Engagement (optional)
4	Marriage (optional)	Marriage

As you can see from the illustration above, God's standard is transparent and safely leads a couple to marriage. However, depending on the two individuals, some during courtship having already finalised their future marriage plans; go straight to the wedding day without the proposing phase which is called "engagement". On the contrary, the world's standard is very uncertain. The woman dating her man sort of hopes that he will propose to her. The man on the other hand, makes that decision to propose to his woman when he finally realises that he wants to spend the rest of his life with her, sadly, he might never come to that realisation. Though some couples reach the engagement stage, according to the world's standards, even after the engagement, this is not an indication that they will marry. Some couples prefer to play husband and wife and even have children whilst they are still engaged. Within the world's standard, the act of sex can to be explored at any one of the four stages. The world's standard have no boundaries, whereas, within God's standard the act of sex is only reserved for the marriage stage, which is the last stage.

Clearly the world's standard poses a lot of risks coupled with folly, for how can one enter a relationship and be willing to give their heart and in most cases give their body too through kissing, touching or sex; wasting away their money, time and emotions without the security of the life long commitment of a marriage? Christians are called to live a life that does not conform to the world's standards (see Romans 12:1-2). Dear reader, are you living your love life like the world does? Is your love life conformed to the standards of the world or surrendered to the standards of the Word of God? Why don't you choose to trust God today with your love life?

God desires you to have a stress-free and happy love life but you can only attain such blessings when you abide in Him and His Word. Choose Jesus today, choose His ways!

Dating vs Courting

Single-hood should be a time to develop a deep and personal relationship with God and building one's own personal skills, gifts and character but sadly this generation of single males and females are purposely piercing themselves with many dilemmas because of dating. It is sad because Satan is using these important seasons of their lives to engage in youthful lusts, through what media portrays in the films and music videos. As a result, the sensual lifestyle easily appeals to them because they do not have a personal relationship with God in order to know God's standards. We wonder why there is so much divorce in our generation as compared to the 1800s and early 1900s. Some of it is due to this model of "dating" which was meant for good but is actually causing more harm than good. Dating causes early emotional promiscuity because one gives away pieces of their heart in each dating relationship until there is very little left for that one and only husband or wife that they will spend the rest of their life with. Dear reader, do you think it is right or healthy for you to have an emotional attachment with different men or women every month or year? Certainly not, but this is what multiple dating relationships do; surely there is a gross error with this Dating model.

Our culture is deceitfully teaching our singles to engage in multiple dating relationships as though this practice will somehow makes them more equipped and knowledgeable about the opposite sex, as if dating is the only means to get to know a person. Certainly not! Dating is not the only engine that can supply information to know a person, more subsequently, friendship is the best engine that can supply sober information about someone. I say this because when people date, they hide most of their faults and put their best foot forward, giving off a false impression about themselves so as to make the other person keep liking them. They present a flawless facet of themselves until they can secure the heart of the other person and in other cunning cases secure the bank account or sexual consent of the other person.

Whereas in friendships, people are more at ease to be themselves as they have nothing to lose or gain. Dating is far from God's original plan for a relationship.

The biblical standard when it comes to having a relationship is called "Courtship". Courtship is the biblical conduct for a relationship leading up to marriage. Whenever two people enter a relationship with a unified agreement of it leading to marriage; this is called courting. Marriage is the core foundation of this type of relationship. In courtship there is no romantic interaction until you are in covenant (married). Sensual acts like kissing, fondling, intimate hugging and sex are reserved for marriage. This type of a relationship is serious and is defined from the beginning; a couple courts in order to see if there is any reason why they *shouldn't* get married. Therefore, you don't go into a relationship because you don't want to work and need someone to pay your bills and leisure costs; you don't enter into a relationship because you want someone to kiss you and have sex with you; you don't enter into a relationship because you need someone to talk to at night and all your friends seem to be relationship goals on Instagram. No... you enter a relationship when you are ready for marriage!

A relationship is not just a thing to have in order to get by through boredom, laziness or loneliness; it should be used to build a pure and holy pre-marriage foundation that the couple can stand on with confidence in marriage.

Moreover, those who enter a relationship should not allow the excitement of being together dazzle them from building a foundation of forgiveness, patience, kindness, communication, trust, selflessness, purity, holiness and love; to carry into their marriage. This is why relationships have to be serious and marriage visioned and not be entered out of convenience but rather out of relevance. Unfortunately, dating makes no room for a couple to prepare and build for marriage until their dating relationship is defined as leading towards marriage; whereas courtship makes room to prepare and build for marriage. However, those who do decide to take the route of courtship still need to court in wisdom without adopting the immature ways of dating. It is very possible for a couple to be in courtship but behave like they are dating. This is because some couples spend their time in courtship dazzled and beguiled by feelings and emotions such that weighty differences, deeply rooted childhood habits, background mindsets, life experiences and future plans are not, to an extent, thoroughly discussed, prayed on or exposed. For example, a couple can become engaged and reach the point of receiving premarital counselling 3 months before their wedding only to discover that the woman doesn't want to have as many kids as the man wants; or that the couple doesn't know about each other's sexual history and sexual health; or that the couple don't know each other's current financial status like debts, loans and credit; or that the man doesn't want his future wife to continue working after she becomes his wife; or that they don't know each other's top 5 ambitions or goals in life. Such couples spent their courtship neglecting the bricks and mortar that build their relationship and future marriage. What a disaster when couples spend their courtship kissing, touching, dining or talking 'sweet nothings' to each other without discovering each other materially, intellectually, emotionally and psychologically. What a tragedy when God puts two people together for marriage but the two don't prepare before marriage by creating a conducive foundation that will aid them to adapt, suit and compliment each other as they build their marriage in unity. Couples should not reach the point of getting engaged without knowing such information about each other.

Though pre-marital counselling is very important, it should not take premarital counselling to discover the past, present and future about the person you are courting to spend the rest of your life with!

Dear reader, are you currently in a courtship? If so, keep in mind that a courtship is meant to help you discover reasons why you should NOT marry that person, not reasons why you should marry them. Entering into courtship is saying I have found reasons to get married to you and I want this relationship to validate those reasons as we head together towards marriage; this is why courtship is serious. It is not like dating, for those who date do so to find reasons why they should marry that person. Hence, when you court or are being courted, you seek out as much marriage focused information as you possibly can find prior to marriage i.e. how they behave when they are angry, how they talk about their enemies, how they treat strangers, how they deal with conflict. A wise courting couple, use their relationship as an opportunity to discuss, prepare and build on differences, opinions, mindsets, goals and visions, such that they can come to a point of compromise or agreement within their differences prior to their wedding day.

For example, if the man is called to be a pastor but the woman hates the idea of being a pastor's wife, a wise couple discusses this in the early stages of their courtship, settles and comes to a compromise or agreement regarding this before they engage. This creates peace and harmony towards their wedding day and when they enter into marriage because there are weightier issues that every married couple will encounter in the battlefield of marriage; issues that will need a prepared and strong foundation. Hence, concerning this example, if a courting couple cannot agree on such a matter, they should not engage.

If you court without building on 1 Corinthians 13:4-8, you will see that in marriage you will need to still go back to work and build what was not built because in marriage you now need to make daily use of what you prepared. A ring, 500 guest wedding, material assets and children will not make the work go away but these will only intensify the pressure of a cracky or unfinished foundation. If you don't learn to communicate as friends in courtship this will be intensified in marriage. If you always like having your way in courtship this will be intensified in marriage. If you cannot accept an apology or be the first to say "I'm sorry", this will be intensified in marriage.

A wise courting couple builds a foundation of good communication, forgiveness, selflessness and much more before they say "I do". Such a couple find a broad space to stand on because they built a good foundation before marriage. The couple that spent their courtship living like they are dating, will find no room to stand on when it's time to be selfless, when it's time to communicate in times of disagreements, when it's time to forgive in times of being disappointed. You will usually hear such couples heralding how difficult their first year of marriage was. Such couple like to impose their struggles as a marriage standard because their toilsome personal experience forces them to believe that the first year of marriage is meant to be wearisome. Dear reader, don't believe the struggles of other people and never make someone else's relationship/marriage your standard but believe in the Word of God and make it your standard. For example, if a couple argues almost everyday in their marriage, due to the grace God gave me in the area of love/relationships, I may discern that they don't pray together DAILY in their marriage and likely didn't practice this prior to marriage.

They did not learnt the concept or importance of praying together daily nor witness the power this has on their ability to adapt to each other. The thing with praying together daily is that it comes at the cost of daily forgiveness and selfless love. If a couple is grudging or angry at each other, it's likely that their joint prayer life is under attack, for how can two enemies pray together in love? Although it's never too late for a couple to pray together daily, it is however, very unfortunate when married couples don't pray together daily because they will undoubtedly fall prey to daily disputes that are inspired by Satan. So then, most struggles couples face can usually be traced back to the foundation they built. Dear reader, if you're purposely dating or you are courting, ask yourself what things are you not doing today that you will be required to do tomorrow in your marriage? What things are you not learning today that you will need to practice tomorrow? If you are courting, make sure that you are both spending your time in courtship wisely asking God for grace because what you sow today prior to your marriage will be your harvest in the first years of your marriage - sow wisely. Another term similar to courtship that the bible uses is "Betrothal". Betrothal was more serious than the engagements we now see. It was so serious that if a woman was caught cheating while betrothed to a man, she was called an adulteress and risked being stoned to death. This is proved in Matthew 1:18-20 "***Now the birth of Jesus Christ was as follows: After His mother Mary was betrothed to Joseph, before they came together, she was found with child of the Holy Spirit. Then Joseph her husband, being a just man, and not wanting to make her a public example, was minded to put her away secretly. But while he thought about these things, behold, an angel of the LORD appeared to him in a dream, saying, "Joseph, son of David, do not be afraid to take to you Mary your wife, for that which is conceived in her is of the Holy Spirit".*** Joseph didn't want people to know that Mary was pregnant though she was betrothed to him and so he was secretly planning to divorce Mary quietly! This is how serious betrothal was, it was surety for marriage through the payment of dowry; this is still present today in Jewish and African cultures. The dowry processes are usually quite lengthy but once a man pays dowry for his future bride, she technically becomes his wife according to tradition.

In most cases, couples will wait to have a church wedding in order to get God's blessing before they start living as husband and wife; partaking in the privileges and blessings of being a husband and wife i.e. physical intimacy. The concept of engagement was taken from this model of betrothal, although being engaged is not as serious because a couple who are engaged may not view their engagement as surety for marriage and can at any time break their engagement without going through a process of divorce.

So then, can you see the seriousness of relationships according to God's standards? That both courtship and betrothal are taken to a very high standard by God biblically and how God's way for a relationship has marriage as its focus and destiny? We see that sensual acts are to be spared for marriage and that a relationship should be used as a tool to build the future marriage of the couple. As a result, some people may wonder and ask themselves if it is not a risk to have no romantic interaction before marriage because they fear the possibility of finding out they have no sexual or romantic compatibility for other when they are married. Well according to God's standard, if you are a woman, you are meant to romance only one man and that is your husband! Likewise, if you are a man you are only meant to romance one woman and that is your wife! We should take our sex instructions from God, the maker and inventor of sex. Sex is something that God invented knowing that it never needed previous experience, it is something you get right the first time without any previous experience. Then the devil came along and said people needed pre-marital sexual experience and some went about and obtained it. Those same couples were not able to fully enjoy the beauty of sex in marriage as a result of the sexual sins they partook in before they got married until they received deliverance and healing from God.

Therefore, since many are breaking this command of saving sex for marriage, we are facing a relationship and marriage riot of destruction. For lack of knowledge, true-love is declining and perishing because few people understand that having sex means you become one physically, psychologically and emotionally with that person. Are you going in relationships and behaving inappropriately?

Are you having sex with the person are in a relationship with? Are you dating for the sake of dating without any intention of marriage? Think about it, how many more people will you continue to become one with physically or emotionally before you marry or are given into marriage? Make a decision today to start doing things God's way. Are you willing to surrender your love life to Him and adopt God's way of thinking and doing things regarding your love life? God wants you to enjoy a godly relationship and godly marriage and train you both for a godly marriage but you have to allow Him to do this because God doesn't choose your spouse, you do. Proverbs 18:22 says, "**He who finds a wife finds a good thing, and obtains favour from the LORD.**" Do you agree with this? A man named Jim Elliot said *"God always gives His best to those who leave the choice with Him."* It may still surprise you to know that God likes you to make your own choices within His will. God can point you to His blessings for you but you have the free will to say yes or no. For example, if a friend gives you $1000 today, to enjoy on a holiday in Australia, it is up to you to chose the mode of transport to reach this place. The friend will not force you to go an aeroplane when in growing up, you were accustomed to travelling on boats.

Will you say yes to God's choice? Will you leave the immoral or promiscuous today and take hold of what Christ has for you marriage-wise? If so, say, "Jesus Christ, I repent of living my life according to lustful desires; I surrender to You full ownership of my heart and life today; lead me in Your paths of righteousness for Your Name's sake; create in me a clean heart today and teach me how to be pure in my way of living. I trust You that you will take care of my heart as you prepare me to be godly in my way of living as well as for my future spouse and marriage. I desire a godly marriage LORD Jesus, prepare my future spouse wherever he/she is as you prepare me, in Jesus Name I pray, Amen".

Chapter Five

THE GIFT OF SEX

Sex was created for the husband and his wife to enjoy, their bodies no longer belong to themselves but the body of the wife belongs to the husband and likewise the body of the husband belongs to the wife (1 Corinthians 7:4). Through sex, they completely give themselves to each other in every aspect of their lives through the transparency of nakedness. Hence, sex is like a signature to their oneness, it's a stamp of seal to their oneness. Sex is the affirmation of their unity, commitment and love; holding a similar likeness to that of the wedding rings they faithfully wear daily on their fingers. So then, what can an 18 year old boy and a 15 year old girl (or any other age group who are not married) be affirming when they have sex? What or who's sort of picture and story are they trying to reflect? Outside marriage, sex becomes poisoned, diluted, impure and sinful. In this chapter you will begin to see the biblical principles of sex. By the end of this chapter you will understand the meaning of sex according to God's standard through revelation from the Holy Spirit of God. If you are not yet married you will be able to use this wisdom in your decisions about sex.

Introduction

Sex was designed by God. It is the deepest form of unity that makes "TWO" people "ONE" physically. Hence, it was orchestrated on a foundation of the covenant of marriage between a man and his wife. However, today we live in sex crazed society. It doesn't take too much walking or turning around the corner to encounter a billboard, video, advertisement, book, song, film or conversation that is progressing towards sex. As a result, this society that is unhealthily obsessed with sex is building a pandemonium that has pushed many youths and adults towards the edge of fornication and adultery; all in the defence of tasting the enticements of sex. As a result, many people are having sex but they do not know what sex is! Can we not rightly say that it is madness when one does things they do not understand? The world is obsessively engaging in an activity based on convenience rather than relevance. Not all things that seem convenient are wise to participate in. For example, you are on a cruise ship and you see many groups of people diving into the sea and swimming back to the boat. Do you then also immediately do the same because they are?

Much rather, if you are interested, shouldn't you begin to access yourself and your current circumstances, if this is relevant to you? Can you swim in the sea? Do you know the dangers of swimming in the sea? Do you have knowledge of sea diving? In the same way, it's unwise to have sex because everyone else is doing it. Moreover, It's quite saddening that all what doctors and nurses tell you at the hospitals is to use contraception, use the pill, use a condom, use this and use that; but nobody is telling the little 13 year old or any other age group, that condoms and contraception will not protect against emotional baggages and soul- ties. No one is telling them that safe sex is found only in marriage! To make matters worse, some parents only reiterate to their children what the doctors and nurses are already saying because they themselves do not know the meaning of sex neither! The biggest danger we are now facing is that those in places of influence (doctors, schools and parents), don't know the small print of sex. They cannot see how seemingly small subjects such as kissing fit in the big picture of sex. That sex was created by God and we must therefore take our instructions regarding sex from the Creator and not from Satan who has perverted it through the ages.

What is Sex?

Genesis 2:24 (KJV) says "***Therefore shall a man leave his father and his mother, and shall cleave unto his wife: and they shall be one flesh.***"

1.   The legal and social accountability – Leave

2.   The personal and emotional duty – Cleave

3.   The body and soul union – One flesh

From the above illustration we can see that God does not have a low view of sex, He actually has the highest view of sex. That sexual intercourse is the "final" act of complete self giving and appropriate only in a relationship between two people, a man and a woman in marriage. As God made one man for one woman, the intimacy of sexual intercourse should only be expressed within a responsively loving and committed life-long relationship of a marriage.

Becoming one flesh is an act of complete self giving on both sides of the relationship. Please understand that sex does not make love, but love makes sex. A sexual relationship can never be just a casual affair as this anti-Christ generation proclaims, shunning the principles of God by lightly labelling adultery and fornication as "one night stand" or "affair". The union of sex flows into the whole being of the persons involved as the 2 become 1 person in intimacy; their bodies and souls join together and become one. Hence, sex simply cannot be limited to a small eventful episode that can soon be forgotten; that is a lie from the pit of hell to blind people from seeing the full effects of sex on the body, mind and soul.

Indeed, there are grave consequences that come with having sex before marriage which can be very detrimental if not tackled by the healing of the Blood of Jesus. Once you sleep with a man or woman outside marriage his or her soul connects with yours because by having sex you are proclaiming that you are husband and wife; that you are one. Therefore a soul tie is formed in the spiritual realm and because you proclaimed that you were now one, yet you are not married to that person, this is classified as fornication.

155

Perhaps you are already married but you have sex with someone who is not your husband or wife, a soul tie is still formed with the person you had sex with but this is classified as adultery. The devil who is your accuser uses this sin as a door to come into your life and torment you sexually by assigning a spirit-husband or wife, this is a demon known as incubus or succubus (this is explained more under the topic spirit husbands / wives). Dear reader, do you have sexual soul ties? Have you allowed the Lord Jesus to deliver you from sexual soul ties through repentance? Sometimes a person may wonder why they keep attracting the same kind of wrong men or woman. Well, how can a woman not keep attracting the wrong men when she are still married to Jim, Jarrell and James in the spirit realm? How can a man locate the wife he is hoping or praying for, until the Blood of Jesus divorces his soul from being tied to Cindy, Charlene and Chanice. Three different soul ties competing to destroy him spiritually and emotionally from any relationship he ever has.

Child of God, sin tastes sweet like honey but in the end it bites like a snake and poisons like a viper! For instance, there was a man who lived a very promiscuous lifestyle before he got married. He eventually got married but did not go through a sexual soul tie deliverance. He lied to his fiancee that he was not a Casanova during his bachelorhood years, even despite the wife's inquisitive questions. Now, when they were married, on various occasions whilst having sex with his wife whom I shall call Jane, the husband would start having visions and memories of his previous sex partners and would say under the beguile of the spirit wives, "*Oh, Stella, you are so sweet*". The names would change with each and every sexual encounter with his wife. Just imagine how horrible these moments of truth and embarrassment would be, especially if you misrepresented yourself as having been a chaste guy or lady before marriage? Those who were in fornication must always seek deliverance from soul ties before entering marriage. There is always a consequence for sin but the power of the Blood of Jesus never fails and is always ready to deliver those who are willing to receive deliverance. The power of God is available to renew those who were promiscuous and restore them back spiritually and emotionally (prayer included at the end of this chapter).

The Dimensions of Sex

The Spiritual Part of Sex

⚼ Sex should be sanctified – 1 Thessalonians 4:3-5 says "*For this is the will of God, your sanctification: that you should abstain from sexual immorality; that each of you should know how to possess his own vessel in sanctification and honour, not in passion of lust, like the Gentiles who do not know God;*"

⚼ Wholly and good – Genesis 1:27-28 says "*So God created man in His own image; in the image of God He created him; male and female He created them. Then God blessed them, and God said to them, "Be fruitful and multiply; fill the earth and subdue it; have dominion over the fish of the sea, over the birds of the air, and over every living thing that moves on the earth.*"

⋏ God is Spirit and He created sex – Genesis 1:31 says "***Then God saw everything that He had made, and indeed it was very good. So the evening and the morning were the sixth day.***"

⋏ Sex is to be set apart for marriage only – Proverbs 5:15-17 (AMP) says "***Drink waters out of your own cistern [of a pure marriage relationship], and fresh running waters out of your own well. Should your offspring be dispersed abroad as water brooks in the streets [Confine yourself to your own wife] let your children be for you alone, and not the children of strangers with you.***"

The Body and Soul Part of Sex

⋏ Becoming one – Genesis 2:24 says "***Therefore a man shall leave his father and mother and be joined to his wife, and they shall become one flesh.***"

What Happens To A Woman During Sex

God gave every female a gift that is to be opened by her husband within the environment of marriage, this gift is called a "hymen". This is a thin layer of tissue that fully or partially (depending with the woman) blocks the entrance to the vagina. When a woman who is a virgin has sex for the first time she bleeds because this tissue breaks or tears. However, in some cases this may become damaged due to injures or sports and the woman doesn't bleed when she has sex for the first time even though she is a virgin. In Song of Solomon 4:12 (NIV), it is written concerning this, "**You are a garden locked up, my sister, my bride; you are a spring enclosed, a sealed fountain.**" Hence marriage is a covenant because of the blood shed when the virgin's hymen is torn during sex, it is in this sign that God created marriage to be a covenant. The marriage couple's oneness is sealed by sex, the two have now agreed through her shedding of blood that they are now one in the flesh. The women doesn't bleed every time they have sex but only this once. This signifies that God designed sex to be with one lifelong mate.

God had no intention of a man and woman separating nor divorcing except through death. Hence, only this one man seals this covenant with this one woman. From the beginning, God intended for both the man and woman keep their virginity for each other for their marriage covenant.

Sadly, many primary schools do not teach about the hymen but rather teach about sex in a perverted way that creates a lustful curiosity to young children. In addition to this, we live in an Anti-Christ generation whereby scientists say that this Hymen has no significance because it can tear through vigorous exercise, tampons or masturbation, yet, through knowledge of the Word of God it clearly has a significance! Let's consider the temple of God in the old testament. It had a veil to enter into the Holy of Holies which is also known as the Secret Place, and now in the new covenant this veil has now been removed by Jesus Christ from all born again Christians; the Church (His bride). It's written in Leviticus 16:2 "**and the LORD said to Moses: "Tell Aaron your brother not to come at just any time into the Holy Place inside the veil, before the mercy seat which is on the ark, lest he die; for I will appear in the cloud above the mercy seat.**" and in

Matthew 27:51 which says "***Then, behold, the veil of the temple was torn in two from top to bottom; and the earth quaked, and the rocks were split***". Moreover 2 Corinthians 3:13-14 says "***unlike Moses, who put a veil over his face so that the children of Israel could not look steadily at the end of what was passing away. But their minds were blinded. For until this day the same veil remains unlifted in the reading of the Old Testament, because the veil is taken away in Christ.***" So then, do you perceive how God also gave the woman a hymen to signify the veil that her one and only husband will remove? Marriage between husband and wife is very similar to that of Christ and the Church. Why then should anyone be doubtful or surprised that the hymen has great importance?

Dear reader, if you are woman reading this and still a virgin, I want you to know that this hymen is your wedding "veil"; treasure your virginity! Nowadays, during wedding ceremonies we see brides wearing a veil to cover their faces, this has now somehow lost its significance. This act of wearing a veil was to symbolise the veil of the hymen. To show that your husband is now about to "***know you***" spiritually, emotionally and physically; and he is about to

162

give his strength to you as you both join together for your first time through sex. This is why it is said of Adam in Genesis 4:1 "**...And Adam knew Eve as his wife**", but on the account of David and Bathsheba it says in 2 Samuel 2:24, "**Then David comforted Bathsheba his wife, and went into her and lay with her. So she bore a son, and he called his name Solomon...**". Why do you suppose it says that Adam knew his wife but but David it says he went into his wife? This is because David had already committed adultery with Bathsheba before she became his wife when she was another man's wife. Therefore, daughter of God, your virginity is not a fashion or a trend. It's not something you throw away because all your friends are having sex and laughing at you because you are not like them. It's not something you lose care in because Rihanna, Beyonce or Nicki Minaj are not singing about it. It is not something you take lightly because you think there are no longer any men who are virgins like you because the truth is there are many men who are still virgins like you. Therefore, your virginity should not be dependant on someone else's but rather depend on honouring God. Your virginity is a weapon against Satan in marriage! It's also a blessing waiting to be inherited in marriage by your husband.

163

It's for you in as much as it is for your future husband. Lastly and more importantly, it's also not for you to idolise or become prideful of.

What Happens To A Man During Sex

An equally significant aspect concerning virgins is that, the man who is a virgin when he unites with his wife for the first time in marriage through sex, he will "*know her*" because he is correctly aligned by his sexual purity and marriage to her to "know her". Hence, he inherits the blessing of adapting to her, complementing her and being suited to her needs and wants. This is a blessing illustrated in Genesis 2:18 AMP which says, "**Now the LORD God said, It is not good (sufficient, satisfactory) that the man should be alone; I will make him a helper meet (suitable, adapted, complementary) for him**". God wasn't simply talking about what He wants to do but also illustrating that He is choosing one woman for the man, and that after the man waits for her, he'll enjoy the blessing of being suitable, adapted and complementary for her in marriage. This sort of man has a special "favour" upon him, as compared to the one who has had sexual relations before marriage andis not yet healed or delivered. When a man is not delivered from sexual soul-ties he is hindered from "knowing his wife" because he polluted himself sexually by knowing other women.

Such a man will gradually see that after the honeymoon period fades, he is finding it difficult to understand his wife; he will become confused about her. This is because he has not yet been healed and delivered from all the soul ties he has when he discovered other women sexually. This is how many couples end up continually arguing in marriages, 50% of the time this is due to soul-ties that were carried into their marriage and were not dealt with before the couple entered marriage. When men and women marry whilst they are still sexually contaminated with sexual soul ties, they are not in a position to truly enjoy their marriage until they get totally healed; until the wounds and scars from the previous sexual relations are healed; until they are delivered from baggages and soul ties from previous relationships. Do you know that it is possible to have a peaceful marriage with very few arguments; to have disagreements and still have peace? God desires couples to experience great joy, peace and harmony in marriages but the enemy tries to steal these blessings mainly through previous pre-marital relationships that invited baggages and soul ties into a marriage.

Dephne Madyara

Each time a man has sex with a woman he gives her part of his strength and energy. During the process of sexual intercourse there is a transfer of strength that occurs from man, not only physically (through ejaculation) but also emotionally and spiritually. Many men and some woman think that it is only necessary for the woman to remain a virgin for marriage and really necessary for the man, not knowing that both the man and woman need to equally wait and remain as virgins for their future spouse. The man especially needs to save his strength for his wife, his seed (sperm) for his wife, his sexual energy for his wife; it's written in Proverbs 31:3 (NKJV), *"Do not give your strength to women, nor your ways to that which destroys kings..."* This is why some husbands who spent their youth having sex with different women are now too tired (have a lower sex drive) for their wife, they have explored every (moral) possible sexual act of pleasure before marriage and now they have lost the novelty to un-presumably discover their covenant wife; this is why after 0-2 years of marriage some husbands are already sexually bored by their wife by allowing the enemy to make them long for their previous sexual escapades; this is why there is comparison and insecurity in some marriages as one

167

spouse consistently tries to live up to the sexual, physical or emotional expectations of the other spouse's previous experiences. Satan knew the implications that premarital sex has on marriage, that's why he gets men at very young ages to start exploring sex and lies to them that this will make them stronger when in reality it makes them weaker because they lose themselves in women they have no future with and blocks their future 'marriage-bed' blessings. The devil knows the power that holy, whole and pure sex has on a marriage. Dear man of God, there is a blessing in waiting for your wife! Wait for your wife! Ask God to give you grace to be chaste for your wife and God will give you grace.

Indeed, there is a blessing that comes with waiting for marriage, a blessing that money cannot buy. In as much as there are curses attained through sex outside marriage, there are also marriage blessings attained through sex, which God preserved for those who are faithful to wait until marriage and those who are healed and walk in purity.

In this way, because of the differences between men and women, these blessings will be fulfilling, joyful and praiseworthy. For example, women and men are different in that women tend to be emotional while men are more inclined to be rational. In an average situation a woman is most likely to react to a situation based on how she feels emotionally at that particular moment, whereas, a man would react to it based on facts or reason. As a result, the sexual blessings inherited in marriage are intended to ease these differences so that the two sort of adapt and compliment each other easily because they are being made one through sex not only physically but also emotionally and spiritually (their souls), without the resistance of a spirit husband or wife; soul ties nor baggages. This is the power and beauty of sex, to know each other as your souls are being tied together. Therefore, sex is too precious and far too valuable to be wasted on a vagabond (one who wanders from place to place not having a permanent home). I say this with great sadness and compassion for you, may these words sink into your spirit and soul that "sex is too expensive to be given to anyone other than your own husband / wife.

It is worthy of only one person in your whole entire life, and that is your wife or your husband." Choose today to be chaste and to honour this command in 1 Corinthians 6:18-20 (KJB), *"Flee fornication. Every sin that a man does is outside the body; but he that commits fornication sins against his own body. What? know you not that your body is the temple of the Holy Spirit who is in you, whom you have of God, and you are not your own? For you are bought with a price: therefore glorify God in your body, and in your spirit, which are God's."*

Types of Soul-Ties

In the book of 1 Samuel 18:1, this verse our understanding on soul tying / knitting as it says "***Now when he had finished speaking to Saul, the soul of Jonathan was knit to the soul of David, and Jonathan loved him as his own soul.***" The Hebrew word used for knit is "*QASHAR*" and the Hebrew word used for soul is "*NEPHESH*".

1.   **Qashar** means to bind, tie, bind together, league together, conspire

2.   **Nephesh** means soul, self, life, creature, person, appetite, mind, living being, desire, emotion, passion.

Can you see the great depth of what is involved in the process of soul tying? Your appetites, mind, life, being, desires, emotions and passions become bound and tied together with another person's. God wasn't kidding around when He created sex; The Word of God certainly was not joking when it said in Genesis 2:24 (NLT) "***...and the two are united into one.***"

Sex really makes the 2 become 1 not only physically and emotional but also spiritually (in regards to the soul), irregardless of whether the persons' involved are participating in it legally through marriage or not.

How Soul-Ties Are Formed

During Sex:

1. A godly soul tie is formed when a man and woman become one sexually in marriage according to Genesis 2:24.

2. An ungodly soul tie is formed during sex outside marriage be it adultery or fornication as Jeremiah 3:1a says, **"If a man divorces his wife, and she goes from him and becomes another man's, may he return to her again? 'Would not that land be greatly polluted? But you have played the harlot with many lovers..."** Sex outside marriage in God's eyes is sin, therefore this ungodly soul-tie that forms during sex opens a door that enables a demon called a spiritual husband/wife to enter that person's life and become one with the fornicator or adulterer in the spirit realm.

Habitually Close Companionships:

Like the example of David and Jonathan, godly soul ties between friends, enable productivity and fruitfulness of both parties in certain areas of their lives. Whereas ungodly soul ties between friends give room for manipulation and stagnancy to take place in that person's life. Therefore, it is essential for male and females to know their boundaries when communicating with the opposite sex no matter the circumstances and how lonely they may feel. This is because feelings are usually manifestations of thoughts; it is crucial for one to discern the source of their thoughts. Proverbs 4:23 says "***Keep your heart with all diligence for out of it spring the issues of life***". This is because when there is no self-discipline and boundaries, there is an open door for an emotional soul-tie to take place between the man and the woman. In most cases women are emotional more emotional than men and may easily open-up their hearts to a man which can lead to an emotional soul -tie if not controlled. Friendships with the opposite sex need discretion because without that, one will not be able to recognise the forming of an emotional soul-tie until it is too late and their regular conversations and meet-ups change into regular kissing, touching and sexual sessions.

Dear reader, have you fallen prey to an emotional soul tie with a friend of the opposite sex due to lack of boundaries?

Your innocent conversations turned into lustful discussions? You regular hang out days turned into romancing sessions? How does this happen? It happens when you don't set personal boundaries. You must "always" set boundaries in your "mind" that you abide by; boundaries that align with God's word. Hence why it's important to renew your mind daily through God's Word as written in Romans 12:1-2, "*I beseech you therefore, brethren, by the mercies of God, that you present your bodies a living sacrifice, holy, acceptable to God, which is your reasonable service. And do not be conformed to this world, but be transformed by the renewing of your mind, that you may prove what is that good and acceptable and perfect will of God.*" and 2 Corinthians 10:4-5 (KJV) "*For the weapons of our warfare are not carnal, but mighty through God to the pulling down of strong holds;) Casting down imaginations, and every high thing that exalteth itself against the knowledge of God, and bringing into captivity every thought to the obedience of Christ*".

So then, when you have a mind depraved of God's wisdom you are likely to be in this category of example; if you are a woman and think to yourself in your heart "today, I want to wear tight jeans and a low cut top that John may notice my body"; that is an example of lack of discretion. By thinking like this, you have already crossed the friendship boundary in your heart and mind because you have intentionally planned to make John lust after your body by wearing that top that spills out your cleavage whilst revealing your navel area and those jeans that enticingly expose the shape of your bum and even your underwear. Remember, he is not your husband, he is just your friend (a brother in God's eyes), he is like your own brother, therefore respect him and protect him, because men are visual. If your motive is to get John to like you or notice you as a potential love interest, it's likely John will only end up more interested in your body than in the real you. Therefore, boundaries begin in the mind! Building a godly mindset through God's wisdom is essential for every believer because this gives you power to decide how far you will go in certain conversations; how far you are will to go in certain embraces, certain gestures and in particular if you are a woman, how you dress around your male friends etc.

A foolish man or woman has no boundaries, he or she says anything to their friend of the opposite sex, he or she playfully touches them anywhere and let's them do the same, he or she flirts with them but wonders why they are acting funny or indirectly suggesting sexual favours.

So then, to conclude, soul-ties are mainly formed by sex and spending a lot of time together with someone; either a friend or acquaintance. There are other ways that soul ties are formed, however, sex and habitually close relationships are the most common ways that soul ties form in regards to relationships. If you want to know more about soul-ties I have a book called '**Breaking Soul Ties - the deliverance manual**" which teaches extensively on all types of soul ties, how they form, the effects they can have on you and includes prayers on how to break them.

The Spirit Husband / Wife

A spiritual husband or wife is a demon also known as incubus or succubus. The succubus is a demon manifesting itself in the form of a woman whereas the incubus is a demon manifesting itself in the form of a man. Their role is to drain out your energy including the fruits of the Holy Spirit and exhaust you by polluting your virtues. Unless one repents and gets delivered these spirits continue to cause havoc in any relationship this person enters in or in a marriage.

Unfortunately, there is no spiritual or emotional condom for sex. A condom may act as a prevention from STD's or HIV/AIDS but it surely cannot prevent emotional baggages, traumas and soul -ties. Since soul-ties influence the feelings, desires, appetites, thinking, passions and emotions of a person, many fornicators and adulterers may not realise that when they engage in sex before marriage or outside marriage they partake and inherit that person's evil ways. For it is written in 1 Corinthians 6:16 (NLT), "***And don't you realise that if a man joins himself to a prostitute, he becomes one body with her? For the Scriptures say, "The two are united into one***".

Certainly, there is no shortage of disagreement that there is always a sense of confusion or emptiness after having sex outside marriage, due to the fact that you have inherited a new evil thing. A spirit husband / wife alters your mind, intellect, will and emotions. Dear reader, since having premarital sex, do you suddenly find yourself having jealous outbursts, insecurities, a new character or new interests that you never had before? It could be a result of the soul-tie, for example, if the person you slept with enjoyed vampire or horror films you will soon find yourself gravitating towards this interest. It is because their soul and your soul became one when you had sex. This is why sex is only safe in marriage.

As a consequence of sexual sin, a spirit husband / wife comes to drain out your energy in different areas of your life through having sex with you in dreams. The spirit husband or wife can come in a dream with the likeness of your other half or even someone whom you trust in order to deceive you. This demon is so lewd that it can even come in your dream posing as your father, mother or brother trying to have sex with you. For instance, a pastor lived with his family and one of his daughters at a high security complex. The daughter was being sexually molested almost every night by these demons. Since there was no other man in the apartment and security was tight at the apartment, the daughter told the mother and some people at Church that her father was sexually molesting her at night. It was only after counselling and prayer that it was revealed that it was the work of sex demons who would masquerade as the father. Furthermore, the daughter and the mother also admitted that the abuses would sometimes occur when the Pastor (father) was away on preaching errands elsewhere.

Are you experiencing similar instances? When you are asleep you have dreams of someone familiar coming to have sex with you? Child of God, don't listen to the world and what scientists say. It is NOT godly and should NOT be acceptable to have sex with anything or anyone in dreams or through masturbation. Sex was created to be a physical enjoyment between a man and his wife in their physical bodies. This is why believers should always plead the blood on their minds because Satan being the coward that he is, cannot attack you physically but does so when you are unaware; when you are sleeping.

Therefore, be alert, the spirit husband / wife can gain access into a person's life not only through fornication or adultery but also through other sexual sins such as masturbation, pornography and emotional adultery (having romantic feelings for numerous men or women). Sins such as masturbation and pornography cloud the mind with lust making it easier for sin to breed, these create an enabling sinful environment for emotional adultery; opening doors for the entry of sex demons of incubus and succubus. Do not let the wisdom of this world, through psychology or psychiatry or any other person, tell you that masturbation is not a sin – it is a sin; or that wet dreams are a natural biological or physiological reaction, 99.9% of the time they are not. They are caused by spirit wife or spirit husband that will be having sex with the victim in dreams.

There are three types of sex dreams associated with these sex demons, from the least lethal to the most lethal:-

1.   One in which you realise you have been sexually abused in your sleep and you know it without a shadow of doubt and can see the evidence of the emissions when you wake up just after orgasm or later in the morning.

2.	The second one, you totally forget or never remember the nocturnal demonic sex encounter in the dream, but you only see evidence of emissions in your nether regions.

3.	The most dangerous of them all is that you do not suspect or experience any sex during the night and you don't remember the dream at all and never see any evidence of the same during the morning because the sex demons would have collected your emissions for use in the spirit world. At least with the first two demonic sex encounters, you know something is wrong and you can do something about your deliverance, but with the third, you can't diagnose the problem, let alone the solution, however fear not, in due course, the Holy Spirit will always reveal all truth to the children of God. Perhaps this book is a step to knowing that truth.

Meditation

Firstly, before we enter into warfare prayer for sexual sins, let's first meditate on the Word of God in Isaiah 53:4-5 and Colossians 2:13 -15, in order to see what Jesus did for you through the cross and how you are now freed from all troubles and battles that oppose you in any area of your life.

Therefore Isaiah 53:4 says "**Surely He has borne our griefs and carried our sorrows; yet we esteemed Him stricken, smitten by God, and afflicted.**" o mean Jesus Christ the Son of God who is glorified and now sits at the right hand of God the Father bore your griefs and sorrows as He carried the cross to Calvary. This is your deliverance. Believe by faith in Jesus that you are no longer a victim of grief and sorrow. You now have the power through His name to command grief and sorrow to leave in the name of Jesus the Christ. Amen.

Isaiah 53:5a says "**But He was wounded for our transgressions..**" What are these transgressions? In Hebrew the word used for transgressions is "Pasha" to mean rebellion or trespass. Amen! Jesus the Christ, who is the Lamb Without Blemish took away your transgressions

183

when He bled after they nailed His feet and hands onto the Cross. By His blood, transgression no longer has power over you, but you have power over transgressions in the name of Jesus. Believe and take hold of this Truth by faith in Jesus because He has set you free!

Isaiah 53:5b says "*He was bruised for our iniquities...*" This Scripture is confirmed in John 19:34 which says "*But one of the soldiers pierced His side with a spear, and immediately blood and water came out.*" Therefore what is iniquity? It is sin that runs in the blood (generational, hereditary). For example, you might find that certain families have a string of cancer deaths. Cancer is just a demon that entered due to iniquity in that family from generation to generation. Continuing on, they bruised His side with a spear, and blood and water came out. Therefore, in the name of Jesus, iniquity has no access to you and what so ever power/throne of iniquity in your family, it cannot run in your blood because you were bought by the Blood of Jesus. Iniquity has to pass through the blood of Jesus first, of which nothing can! Believe that you are freed by faith in Jesus' name. No longer do generational curses, roots and patterns have hold over you.

When you pray speak up and say by the blood of Jesus I address you thrones of iniquity in my family and life, be rooted out, be pulled down, be destroyed, be thrown down into the pit of hell in the of Jesus the Christ!

Isaiah 53:5c says "*the chastisement for our peace was upon Him and by His stripes we are healed*". Every stripe laid upon Jesus was noted for every kind of sickness, 39 stripes in total for all sicknesses known to mankind. Therefore, for every sickness Jesus paid the price by His blood. When you pray address every sickness you have by the blood of Jesus saying "you (insert name of sickness e.g. H.I.V) I address you by the blood of Jesus the Christ to leave my body and be thrown into the pit of hell and never again return here on earth in the name of Jesus the Christ, because by the stripes of Jesus I "WAS" healed, therefore you no longer have any access to enter my body nor any part of my life!" Amen.

To summarise Isaiah 53:4-5:

1. HE HAS BORNE – the Hebrew word used is "NASA" meaning "*to lift, bear up, carry, take*", therefore He lifted and carried off your griefs as He carried the Cross.

185

2.   HE CARRIED – the Hebrew word used is "CABAL" meaning *"to bear, bear a load, drag oneself along"*, therefore He was able to bare the load of all your sorrows, taking them away.

3.   HE WAS WOUNDED – the Hebrew word used is CHALAL meaning *"to profane, defile, pollute, desecrate, begin"*, therefore He was polluted and defiled for your transgressions.

4.   HE WAS BRUISED – the Hebrew word used is DAKA meaning *"to crush, be crushed, be contrite, be broken"*, therefore He was crushed for your iniquities.

5.   THE CHASTISEMENT – the Hebrew word used is "MUWCAR" meaning *"discipline, chastening, correction"*, therefore the discipline and correction for your Peace was upon Him.

6.   AND BY HIS STRIPES – the Hebrew word used is "CHABBURAH" which means *"bruise, stripe, wound, blow"*, therefore by His blows and bruises you are healed.

Lets meditate on Colossians 2:13 which says, "**And you who were dead in trespasses and in the uncircumcision of your flesh (your sensuality, your sinful carnal nature), [God] brought to life together with [Christ], having [freely] forgiven us all our transgressions**"
When you were not yet saved you did various sinful things because you were dead to righteousness and holiness, but very much alive to unrighteousness and sin. However, when you received salvation, your spirit man was made alive by the Holy Spirit power of God through Jesus Christ and all those sins no matter how big or small, were forgiven and by faith you have access to this forgiveness. All you have to do is believe that Jesus forgave you, which this Scripture rightfully says that Jesus freely forgave you. You don't have to feel forgiven; you were forgiven.

Colossians 2:14 (AMPC) says "**Having cancelled and blotted out and wiped away the handwriting of the note (bond) with its legal decrees and demands which was in force and stood against us (hostile to us). This [note with its regulations, decrees, and demands] He set aside and cleared completely out of our way by nailing it to [His] cross.**"

This "handwriting of note" are things that manifest due to sin, for example, due to fornication or adultery the sin manifests a spirit husbands /wives. Another example is, due to alcohol abuse the lack of self control manifests as a liver disease. Another example is that due to previously having been cheated on in a relationship this manifests as fear and insecurities. All these manifestations have been cancelled by the Blood of Jesus. The Blood of Jesus is living as His Word, it is powerful and it cancelled the tightest bonds of Satan; it blotted out the deepest inscriptions of Satan carved into your life due to past sins. All you have to do is address everything by the Blood of Jesus believing and knowing that those things were already cleared out of your way. The thing with Satan is that he needs to be told, otherwise he simply won't leave you or let go of your blessings in Christ. You have the authority to tell him and his demons through the Blood and name of Jesus.

Colossians 2:15 says, "*[God] disarmed the principalities and powers that were ranged against us and made a bold display and public example of them, in triumphing over them in Him and in it [the cross].*" Indeed powers and principalities were disarmed!

188

The Greek word used for DISARMED means *"wholly put off, despoil, disarm"*. All power of Satan is now under your feet because the LORD Jesus crushed Satan and made you rule over him in Jesus' name. It's written in Luke 10:19, **"Behold, I give you the authority to trample on serpents and scorpions, and over all the power of the enemy, and nothing shall by any means hurt you."**

Warfare Prayer

Before you begin this prayer concerning soul-ties, it is according to Colossians 2:13-15 and Isaiah 53:4 -5; and having meditated on these Scriptures, you now know that through the Blood shed on the Cross all troubles and evil against you were already disarmed and you were healed when you received salvation. This prayer is to remind the devil and his powers that you are now in charge, and under the unction of the Holy Spirit they must leave! Just begin to ask the Spirit of God saying "Holy Spirit of God, the Revealer of all things I ask you in the name of Jesus that you begin to identify and show me every ungodly soul-tie that has been formed in my life and every person in my life whom I have an ungodly soul-tie with. Holy Spirit my

Helper by Your power, severe out every ungodly soul-tie out of my life. Thank you Holy Spirit for the transformation and purification you are beginning to do in my life. Amen."

As the Holy Spirit begins to reveal to you and bring to remembrance all the ungodly soul-ties, if they are a result of sin, prepare yourself and confess them to the LORD and repent (if you haven't already repented) for it is written in Proverbs 18:21, "*life and the death are in the power of the tongue...*" and Matthew 16:19 which says "*And I give you the keys of the kingdom of heaven, and whatever you bind on earth will be bound in heaven, and whatever you loose on earth will be loosed in heaven.*" Begin to renounce every ungodly soul-tie in your life saying "By the Blood of Jesus and the power of the Holy Spirit of God I address every ungodly soul-tie and spirit husband (or wife) I renounce (insert name or names of the persons you slept with) out of my life and divorce you right now by the blood of Jesus Christ you are now disarmed and by the Holy Spirit power of God I destroy you. You unclean spirit, you are no longer spiritually, emotionally or physically tied to me because by the Blood of the Lamb without Blemish, your handwriting of requirements that were against me and contrary to me, were wiped off and blotted out; taking you out of my way and life. In the name of Jesus go! Go to the pit of hell and never again return here on earth! Amen."

Chapter Six

The KILLERS of DESTINY and RELATIONSHIPS – *an equipment for your journey*

Dephne Madyara

Nowadays we live in a society that specialises in forced domination. Whereby it has become acceptable to push people out of the way to reach the place of number 1. We see this in popular ad campaigns, in films, in music videos and unfortunately this mindset has infiltrated the Church. It seems that the society is teaching us that "to get higher in life you must destroy everyone that's in your way by whatever means!" Judging this movement spiritually you can indefinitely trace the spirit behind this. It is manipulative and controlling, and it cannot be subjected to authority. By the end of this chapter you should be able to discern the character and tactics of a Jezebel spirit, a Athaliah spirit, a Delilah spirit and Amnon. Looking at your own heart, your close female and male companions you will be able to see traces of this spirit. Above all let the Holy Spirit open your eyes. Amen.

Introduction

Throughout the bible we see 3 influential women with a related character.

1) Jezebel who is assigned to destroy one's present time

2) Athaliah who is assigned to destroy one's future

3) Delilah who is assigned to slowly drain and rob one's strength or anointing.

They are a three evil cord and can at times work together in an individual or separately. They may also influence a person's actions externally. Sadly, because the times we live in are evil, these three spirits are genderless and operate in both women and men. The main purpose being to destroy marriages, relationships, families, friendships, churches, destinies, breakthroughs and blessings whether in the present time or future. Furthermore, there is also one spirit among men which is closely seen in what they call "a player" this is the spirit of Amnon, which seeks to rob and kill a woman's innocence, femininity and virtues.

Dephne Madyara

The Spirit of Jezebel

The name Jezebel is spelt in Hebrew as *"LYZEBEL"* and it means "*Baal exalts, un-husbanded one, without cohabitation and unchaste*". This spirit hates authority, hates being subjected and loves attention. Though I refer to Jezebel as "she" in some instances, Jezebel is genderless and can operate in both men and women, with or without their knowledge.

Its Traits and Character

⅄ Jezebel hates authority hence why her name means "Un-husbanded one". For someone to have a husband they'd have to be willing to submit to their husband. However, Jezebel does not submit to anybody but Satan. She sees herself as the king and leader of the house. Her influence is depicted by Hollywood and MTV. Whereby a women is walking around nearly naked, holding a leash that's chained onto a man's neck to show that he is under her control (I have seen this in a music video by Rihanna called S&M which was banned in 11 countries). Furthermore we have young little girls and grown women mimicking and lifting up hands to songs like "girls run the world by Beyonce". Such things are not innocent and the wisdom depicted in those songs, videos, campaigns etc is not from God but is sensual and demonic. It's a movement inspired by the spirit of Jezebel and Delilah.

⚴ Jezebel hates men and women in authority who are over her position. She will do just about 'anything' to get someone's place of prominence.

⚴ This spirit especially hates men of God who are faithfully doing the work of God. She will come in that church to pollute it and quench the flow of the Holy Spirit. If she goes in a weak church, there will begin to be little revelation of God's word during sermons and there will barely be any testimonies. That church would need to be strong in prayer. If you are in ministry and not yet married it is very important that you walk in the gift of discernment because the devil will try and pair you up with a Jezebel partner to infiltrate your anointing, calling and influence. It will usually be someone who is knowingly or unknowingly involved in forms of witchcraft, in order to make sure that you quench the Holy Spirit.

⋏ Jezebel hates the Truth and those who speak it, such that she will hold any idle word or action incurred, against them. She seeks to destroy those who openly speak the Truth, especially if the Truth exposes her ugly ways and motives.

⋏ A Jezebel spirit in a woman will not submit to a man, if she does it will only be in pretence in order to gain ground or favours; her submission is conditional. Some wives allow this spirit to entice them and they end up submitting to their husband only when it is beneficial to them; this is rebellion in the marriage bed.

⋏ A person with a Jezebel spirit may look innocent and be widely known as being very helpful and friendly, but he/she is deceitfully cunning and subtle; likely trying to gain ground and favour.

⋏ A Jezebel places themselves in the place of prominence subtly and by craftiness with objectives of popularity, if possible even to the degree of being worshipped. Those with a Jezebel spirit long to be praised and adored like a god. When a church is run by a leader with a Jezebel spirit, that leader will be worshipped by the congregation and he/she will encourage it indirectly usually through manipulation. The leader will not do anything to stop people from worshipping them. Apostle Paul did great works for God to the point where people's admiration of him was slowly turning into an obsession and worship but he discouraged this in this account written in Acts 14:11-15.

⚔ A Jezebel never forgets when they are wronged because they struggle to forgive others. Therefore, he/she will not be at peace until they find revenge, even if it takes years to achieve. Jezebels do not forgive nor forget.

⚔ A Jezebel is secretly compulsive and desperately stalks those he/she envies, being obsessive in finding every single piece of detail about those he/she hates. The person with this spirit will try and find out even the smallest of details about their opponent to use for a plot.

⅄ A Jezebel has no identity of her own, no real gifts or talents; like a leech they feed off from others by stealing ideas and counterfeiting other people's gifts in order to establish themselves or become popular. If a gifted or talented person has a Jezebel as a friend that person will suffer greatly because Jezebel will act like a friend yet he/she is an enemy seeking to sabotage them and their gifts.

⅄ A Jezebel will volunteer for anything and everything in the church. You will see them participate in 3 or more ministries in the church. They don't do so because they want to help or are called to be there but because they are controlling and want to lead many things for the purpose of receiving admiration. They also don't know their purposeful place in the Body of Christ. This is why leaders in the bible would only choose workers for a ministry area in the Church, after prayer and fasting (even minor ones ministry areas like food distribution). Jezebels can quickly be discerned when prayer and fasting is involved.

Incorruptible Beauty

⚐ A Jezebel has no close friends but has many friends because he/she is not genuine, trustful nor faithful. He/she knows that they cannot be too close to anyone as this exposes them.

⚐ A Jezebel sits, sleeps and eats plotting ways to destroy those he/she hates and like a snake they carefully watch for an opportune time to strike.

⚐ Those under Jezebel in position whether in the workplace, ministry or family dynamics; will tend to fear him/her because when a Jezebel is in power, he/she has an authoritative and threatening demeanour. He/she will cunningly make you believe that you need him/her and you're nothing without their help.

⚐ A Jezebel thinks he/she can have any man/woman they want, even if the person is already with someone. This is because Jezebel finds a thrill in destroying relationships and feels powerful knowing that another woman's man or another man's woman is giving them attention. A Jezebel in a woman doesn't care if he's your boyfriend or husband. A

Jezebel in a man doesn't care if she's your boyfriend or wife. He/she doesn't respect you nor your relationship and if he/she wants your man/woman, they will do whatever they can to get him/her because the assignment of Jezebel is to destroy the relationship or marriage.

⅄ He/she is the opposite of everything 1 Corinthians 13:4-8 says about Love. A Jezebel is impatient, a show off, proud, rude, selfish, provoking, thinks of evil, rejoices in sin, unbearable, unbelieving and unendurable. However, it takes one who abides in the Word of God to be able to discern this because these actions will be very subtle and unnoticeable.

⅄ If a woman who is influenced by Jezebel doesn't manage to seduce a man she will then play the victim like socio-paths do by making false witness against him that he raped her or tried to rape her. She hates men who are strong enough to flee from sexual immorality. She will be headstrong in trying to destroy those she failed to subdue, even if it takes years to achieve. Hence, the importance of setting boundaries. Never ever be alone in secluded place with someone of the opposite sex unless the Holy Spirit gives you peace about it. Be alert especially if you are a woman. For example, there is a married Pastor who has raped many young women whom he counsels in his home office, a few other pastors know this but no one has prosecuted him yet because no-one believes that this pastor can do such things and there is no evidence. These women he raped had one thing in common – they were physically beautiful. This is the controlling spirit of Jezebel at work, using its position of prominence to destroy other women's lives.

Dear reader, if you know someone has a Jezebel spirit, do not get too close to him/her because they will use your secrets and flaws against you in the future. Be watchful over people who try to be too close to you quickly, for example, within 1 month a person is sharing deep private things with you and wants you to do the same. Be prayerful and discerning with such people. Following the ways of Jezebel by being friends with him/her is like walking in an unequal yoke. You will suffer calamity and unfruitfulness in areas of your life because you will be walking together with someone whose heart devices evil and sows discord among brethren.

⋏ Even if he/she is married, their conscience is seared and they are not programmed to avoid emotional or physical cheating. For example, the spirit of jezebel in a woman will try making moves on your man, yet she has own man, usually because of jealousy especially if you are genuinely happy or blessed in love, Jezebel wants what you have. She wants that happiness, friendship, peace and purity founded in your relationship.

⋏ A Jezebel can also be very spiritual and religious. He/she will make you think they are more spiritually alert than most people. However, he/she has very little revelation of God's Word and His Love. Jezebel will tell you of the many dreams and visions he/she has had but dreams and visions without knowledge of God and God's word are dangerous.

⋏ Listen to his/her statements, theories and words; weigh them up from different sources; they usually are along the same story line but they don't add up. That is because his/her whole dialect is full of lies. A

Jezebel speaks so many lies such that his/her stories end up being confusing. For example, he/she tells you they were on holiday in New York last summer and tells another person they were working in Miami all of last summer.

✧ If you are in a happy relationship, of which God chose you and your partner, Jezebel will be after you. It's important you and the person you're in a relationship with discuss boundaries; who you open up to about your relationship; setting boundaries on whom you accept advice from. Jezebel is always seeking to destroy a relationship. Relationships are like a house and they must have walls. Everyone shouldn't walk in and out of your house. This creates footprints of dust, impurities and delusions. Only the Holy Spirit should have all access. Jezebel is looking to win and destroy a potentially good future marriage. Therefore, for some people you will have to tell them "Excuse me, please take off your shoes before you come in" that is to mean; keep your opinions, judgements, tales and advices; they are not coming in our relationship.

⚔ It's easy for Jezebel to manoeuvre in a relationship that has no unity. When facing a problem it's important to discuss it together before discussing it to a third party. When you discuss with outsiders first, it is very dangerous and can cause premature death on relationships. As a result withholding information from strangers chokes Jezebel, it deprives the person with this spirit from information. Dear reader, never announce your problems or plans on social media because social media is the easiest way for a Jezebel to gain access to you and because a Jezebel is intelligent they will throughly dissect the information to build ways to destroy you.

⚔ The devil has successfully attached the spirit of Jezebel on some of his music artists. You have to be very careful about whom you are listening to these days. Some very popular music artists are operating under the *anointing* of Jezebel. Ezekiel 28:14 says, "***You were the anointed cherub who covers; I established you; you were on the holy mountain of God; you walked back and forth in the midst of fiery stones.***" Satan was also anointed so guard your heart and mind. Let it be led by the Word of God not by musical lyrics of people whom you do not know what they do behind closed doors. Put your trust in God not in man because there is a transference of spirits by what we watch and listen to. Therefore, before you buy that album or download that song. Ask the Holy Spirit if it is worth it.

⚘ Jezebel wants your inheritance. He/she is after what belongs to you, hence, he/she will implement ways to choke out and starve your faith in God from His promises and prophesies. A Jezebel will even do this through false dreams telling you God told them something about you; or that they dreamt of you when God did not tell them anything. For instance, a woman who pretended to be a friend to me was desperately trying to attach herself to my life because she saw into future. She began to play the role of being a friendly advisor even though I didn't ask for advise, she was overly nice and spoke prophetic words to me trying to divert my love life but she didn't know that secretly, I had already seen her in the spirit realm, fasting against me, my future and plans. Do you know that Jezebel can fast

206

against your plans and ideas? Fasting creates power whether good or evil, this is why different religions fast and there are still results - fasting is spiritual. Therefore, those under the attack of Jezebel must always stand firm in prayer and live a pure life unto God. Dear reader, do not accept every dream, prophesy or voice to speak into your life; many are not speaking from the throne of God but from the pits of hell.

⅄ Jezebel can quickly discern pain, depression and sorrow. You can't hide it from him/her because Jezebel is acquainted with evil. Jezebel will however offer a seemingly brilliant but ungodly alternative method of relief; his/her motive being to gain control over you and to be praised.

⅄ A Jezebel promises to fulfil all your forbidden desires and will do so by unjustly ways. These desires are forbidden because they are rejected and disapproved by God in that they do not align with God's Word. Look at those whom you call friends, what advise do they give you? Does this advise agree with God's promises and instructions? When

207

you ask for help, what are the means they use to help you? Jezebels's husband in the bible, king Ahab, desired another man's vineyard and Jezebel promised the king that she would get him the vineyard. She then set up the owner of that vineyard to be falsely accused and stoned to death; afterwards she incited her husband to claim the vineyard saying that the owner was now dead (read 1 Kings chapter 21).

⅄ If a Jezebel is in a woman, she's will open several accounts on social media websites such as Facebook and Instagram to fight you or to steal your other half. If the basis is to steal your man, she will do this in jealousy of your relationship and will feel better about herself if your man is unfaithful. Many marriages have fallen through social media messages between other women's husbands and seemingly innocent strangers who were in fact Jezebels. Those messages turned in emotional soul ties and resulted in adultery. This weapon is usually used by female Jezebels towards women who are in ministry (Jezebel will message the husband) or men who are in ministry (Jezebel will seek guidance from the man in ministry).

⅄ One of his/her weapons is that he/she always looks like they are about to walk on the runway. You have to wonder when and how she/he managed to make herself up so nicely. Even if it's inappropriate, there is no dull day with the person with this spirit. They trust in their looks and use this as a means to gain favour and if Jezebel is in a woman, she will be adorned beautifully from hair, make-up to her outfit. His/her motive behind this is seduction and power. Though there are people who genuinely just like looking good, it will take discernment to perceive this.

⅄ A Jezebel will have a record of your history and especially knows your triumphs and victories. They will however casually bring up in conversations your flaws and weaknesses to mock you or they will bring up your victories as a way to butter you up. Emotional and spiritual humility, will be your shield.

⅄ When a leader who has a Jezebel spirit is in ministry, due to lack of revelation of the truth of God's word, he/she will twist scripture, manipulate the congregation, direct worship to themselves instead of to God and lastly, in some cases he/she will practice subtle witchcraft and divination even by use of biblical principles and Scriptures.

The Spirit of Athaliah

The name Athaliah is spelt in Hebrew as "ÁTHALYAH" which is to mean "*afflicted of the LORD*". This spirit is an enemy of everything that's to do with God's plans and purposes of destiny towards a chosen or anointed child of God, that is every Christian or any leader. In the bible, 2 Kings 11:1-2 shows how this spirit operates, it's written "***When Athaliah the mother of Ahaziah saw that her son was dead, she arose and destroyed all the royal heirs. But Jehosheba, the daughter of King Joram, sister of Ahaziah, took Joash the son of Ahaziah, and stole him away from among the king's sons who were being murdered; and they hid him and his nurse in the bedroom, from Athaliah, so that he was not killed.***"

What had happened there was that Athaliah had a son who was meant to succeed the throne but he died. Please note that when a person with an Athaliah spirit, their life is full of misfortune, hardships and toil; hence, they will try to cause misfortune, hardships and toil in other's people's lives. So then, after learning that her son was dead, she murdered all male descendants to the throne, in order to ensure illegitimate success to the throne except for Joram was was hidden away. At that time Athaliah became the first queen to ever reign on a throne in those days, for 6 years! This spirit hates bright futures and destinies that will bring enlightenment to the world and will by all means try to harm those who have what it desires. This sexless spirit can be traced in the character of Pharaoh who sought to kill all the Hebrew new born sons (Exodus 1:8-22) and Herod the king who sought to kill Jesus (Matthew 2:16). The spirit is very similar to a Jezebel spirit and Athaliah can operate in both men and women with or without their knowledge. His/her task is to terminate you and take your blessings or destiny before you can live it out.

Its Traits and Character

- Athaliah's family background usually has characteristics of idolatry, witchcraft, corruption, bitterness and desolation. There may not be any seed of Jesus in his/her family history or rarely any Christians in his/her family.

⋏ He/she is a future destroyer. Unlike Jezebel who works in the now, Athaliah operates in the tomorrow. He/she is only concerned with destroying your future by destroying you today. Unlike Jezebel who may seek to only steal and/or kill your destiny; this spirit seeks to utterly destroy you and your destiny.

⋏ He/she is a premature death inducer. A person with a spirit of Athaliah will strive to destroy anything God has put in your life, family or around; anything that bears fruit. Athaliah is not after the fruit, he/she is after the tree that's bearing the fruit. He/she is like the destroying locust, such a person will destroy the crop before it can be harvested.

⋏ He/she induces abortion in any fruitful area of one's life. We see it now in this generation that aborts a child every second. This is a spirit of Athaliah, influencing to abort anything that has potential to bless or bring change to the world tomorrow. If you are pregnant and are having thoughts of abortion or are being pressured by a boyfriend or husband, please do not do it, God has a plan and future for that child irregardless of your circumstances. If you cannot be a mother today, please consider other ways of ensuring the well fare of the child i.e. adoption; do not abort the baby. Plead the blood over your thoughts and mind if the enemy starts giving you those thoughts or telling you that you are not ready or not fit to be a mother.

⅄ Athaliah will destroy any trace of hope in you, leaving only devastation and loss. He/she is determined and viciously aims to destroy your future generation, inheritance, vision and future blessings.

⅄ He/she is a breakthrough blocker. Never share to untrusted sources (or even trusted) what you are about to do business wise, relationship wise or any other until you actually do it or are at a secure stage. Elizabeth in the bible, a barren woman who finally got pregnant after many years, instead of shouting her breakthrough on the rooftops, she instead hid her pregnancy for 5 months; learn from Elizabeth in Luke 1:24-25. This spirit operating in people around you will try to block your breakthrough by into your life seductive words that seem wise but will alter your plans and possibly divert you from God's destiny for you through doubt. Don't say to people, I want to open such and such a business until you have finalised everything and are about to open this business. Athaliah will talk you out of great dreams and visions.

⅄ This spirit wants to terminate your gift, your love for God, your business idea, your abilities, your anointing to lead. So he/she comes in your life masqueraded as a rapist, a bully, a violent boyfriend, an abusive father, a debt crisis. This is because you are extraordinary and the devil is using this to drain you and destroy your future.

⅄ He/she is not indiscreet and doesn't give out warning signs unlike Jezebel who tends to be somewhat sloppy and detectable by the average Christian; Athaliah on the other hand comes in quickly to kill and then destroys any trace of your remembrance. He/she eats away anything before it fully develops. Look into your life and begin to discern the people who are purposely destroying

214

you and bringing you only harm.

⋏ Athaliah steals virtues, gifts, talents and blessings from her victims and uses them all for him/herself, he/she gets all the credit for something you toiled hard for. Just being his/her friend will contaminate you and you will find that you no longer have an interest in your education or suddenly feel lazy to go to work; you lose interest in your vision, goals, gifts and talents.

⋏ Athaliah wants to be in your place of destiny. He/she sees how bright your future is and wants to jump on the wagon with you to get there but push and kill you off when you are near to the place of greatness.

⋏ He/she will defend you, walk with you until you become a threat to their success. This person's ugly side will immediately spring out when there is competition.

⋏ He/she's attracted to anyone who has a successful future. This is why gifted or anointed people are attacked severely, it's your future that the devil is after. Athaliah wants to terminate it because you are not ordinary but extraordinary. His/her purpose is to make you give up when you feel swarmed and consumed by tribulations. It's so important to be constantly absorbed in the Word of God and prayer. Protect your future.

⋏ Even after you have sat on your throne of success, business, ministry, marriage or relationship. Athaliah will still try to fight and accuse you even though he/she has lost. If you are married the man of your destiny and dreams but Athaliah is after your marriage, if you are not yet married, the person with this spirit will try to create a disaster on your wedding day, for example, if this is your maid of honour she will burn your wedding dress as she irons it or do anything that create a loss on the wedding day but if the wedding does continue as normal, the maid of honour she still try to sabotage your marriage one way or the other unless you remove them from your life. When the person with this spirit loses they will cry out "treason!", making it look like you cheated your way to what you have today, even though you rightly earned your blessing. However, by the power of the Holy Spirit and Blood of Jesus this spirit can be executed and voided.

Dephne Madyara

The Spirit of Delilah

The name Delilah is spelt in Hebrew as *"DELIYLAH"* which is to mean "*pining with desire*". The meaning of her name is self explanatory. She pins you down with desire! Her whole being, presence, speech, look and action exude "seduction". She makes her victims suffer mentally and physically with desire for her. She is the epitome of a seductress. This spirit of Delilah is assigned to destroy all men and women of prominence, people with a purpose in life, any pastor or leader who is in ministry. The devil sends women to churches who have this spirit to terminate the church and cause the church leader to commit emotional and physical adultery; and fornication. Her role is through the door of relationships or marriages. She uses this engine to find out their strengths so that she can destroy them and draw out the power of her opponent, removing him or her from their place of prominence. Unlike Athaliah who seeks to destroy, Delilah's mission is to make you weak and keep you weak; imprisoned.

Sadly this spirit can be in someone and this person won't realise that they are being used by a spirit of Delilah to destroy others. Though I refer to Delilah as her in the following instances, this spirit is genderless.

Its Traits and Character

- She is highly skilled in taming men through seduction. Even the strongest of lions will be beguiled by her if they do not stay alert in the Spirit. He/she is not lazy she will effectively work hard to tame even the toughest of individuals. Delilah is after people of prominence and uniqueness; people in the spot light, anointed ministers of God and gifted men and women who are in relationships or marriages. Her assignment is to drain your power to remove you in that place of power and make you ordinary like everyone else.

- She will fool you by being in church every Sunday, at every bible study and every all night prayer. She will be punctual and be involved in many if not all church activities as her way to get close to the pastor or church leaders. She wants his head on her lap.

⚔ She loves money. She would choose money over love within a split second. She can also operate as a gold digger but only more wiser than the average gold digger. Moreover, she is sex hungry and filled with ungodly and perverse sensual desires. She seems to know exactly what she wants and it is usually oriented around power, outward appearance and money. She will prey on any such man, whether he is taken or not.

⚔ Day after day, she will keep trying, pursuing and pressuring a man to leave his wife, and to sleep with her, to run away with her or commit any other sin with her. This she will persuade softly until he listens to her voice. It will take a man who truly loves and fears the LORD to overcome her pleas. She is like the Jack of all trades, knowing the tricks, navigations, avenues, points and steps in getting a man's attention. It is only when a man fears the LORD and has humility that he can overcome her ploys.

⚔ He/she will try to get close to your beloved in order to demolish you by gaining his/her confidence through politeness and kindness. Then as time goes by, your beloved may begin to open up about your relationship to Delilah, because Delilah does the same about his/her relationship. He/she will be a "shoulder to lie on" and a "good listener". Little by little a bond will develop and before you know it, the person with this spirit has your man's/woman's heart and cant wait to see or talk to Delilah. Great anointed men like Samson fell because of her.

⅄ He/she will wreck homes, marriages and relationships because of a charming persona, false humility and excellent charisma.

⅄ This spirit is a seducing spirit and the person who has it is skilled in luring and taming men and women. You will find yourself being drawn to this sort of person without any particular reason and wonder why you are so excited to see him/her. It's important to always put on the full armour of God that you may stand because he/she has vast likeable qualities such that it leaves you confused on what you really do like about him/her. They are like a chameleon, fitting everywhere as a perfect person, however, those whom he/she has stung in the past know about Delilah's ugly side.

⚔ Delilah is out to find out where you are strong and how to turn this strength into a vulnerability and weakness. His/her assignment is to take your power, terminate your strengths and imprison you in a jail of weakness, so that you can be idle and ordinary; void of your anointing and gifts.

⚔ When operating in a woman, you will discover that she is very knowledgeable about what men want and need emotionally and physically, hence, she knows how to treat a man like a king. If another woman's man is being targeted by her, if the lady of this man is not treating him like a king, Delilah is more than willing to do so. She'll be willing to do everything that she dosen't, and do it exceptionally well. She knows the vulnerable areas of a man and how to minister to them like a mother holds and comforts her son when he has fallen down. She is polite and gentle. She will not criticise a man because she realises that this causes him to be defensive and to cave. Rather, she is qualified in the language of praise; praise is her native language! She knows every vowel, lyric, synonym of praise to say to a man. You might discern this spirit in a person who praises your other half more than you, even petty things that do not need praise, you will find the person with this spirit praising anyway, it is because this spirit is after your relationship. She especially takes advantage of a situation whereby your other half is not receiving much praise from you. In cases where Delilah is after you, he/she will praise you exceedingly to butter you up to depend on his/her praise.

⅄ He/she is able to make you feel very secure within a short space of time through his/her gentleness, this is because Delilah is gifted in this by building relationships with his/her prey founded on safety, praise, peace and warmth. However her motives for each are the opposite.

⅄ A person with a Delilah spirit that is after you will make you believe that you have some kind of deep connection together and that you were meant to be best friends or marriage partners, even if this is completely inappropriate and you are already with someone. The person with this spirit will indirectly pressure you daily until you believe it. Understand that this spirit is persistent and a person with this spirit will pester you daily with sweet words. Do not think a "No" will stop them from pursuing you. The only way to win is cutting off all lines of communication with the person.

⋏ Delilah is after the favour of God upon you, your family, your business, your marriage. He/she will do all they can through seduction to make sure this favour departs from you and you are bound in shame. This is why Satan normally send a Delilah to a Church, when she finishes her assignment she will leave the church but then rumours will start to swirl and in no time, the truth will eventually come out if the pastor had committed adultery with Delilah. Delilah's goal is to get the pastor to be publicly shamed so as to step down, which eventually creates disruption in the Church.

⋏ Make-up, beautiful hair, sexually revealing clothes and attractive shoes are Delilah's physical armour. Likewise, a man with this spirit will be very well groomed in a sexually attractive way and usually splashing out his money or financial assets. While the believer is told to put on full spiritual armour, Delilah makes powerful influence through his/her image, assets and wealth. Those who love and fear God will be able to subdue this spirit.

ᴧ Another facet of Delilah is that he/she can be direct in their speech by boldly making perverse statements because of a passive character. Regardless of the setting, he/she will directly make known to you that he/she wants to kiss you, date you or sleep with you. Delilah can be in church meeting with you and tell you directly that he/she is attracted to you, then slip his/her phone number in your purse or pocket. Since this spirit is a seducing spirit, it's then up to you to take up this offer or not.

ᴧ Delilah will orchestrate seclusion in order to trap a man/woman into sleeping with him/her. Delilah will make sure that he/she is alone with the man/woman, be it in an office, a house, a carpark etc, so that he/she can seduce his/her victim. If this spirit is in a woman, she will show up intentionally without her clothes on or under dressed, in order to seduce her victim. Only a man who fears God will be able to escape her ploys.

The Spirit of Amnon

As a single woman, one type of a man to look out for and run away from as far as possible is the Amnon type of man (read the whole of 2 Samuel 13). Do not even give him your phone number or attempt to establish some form of friendship because he is discreetly manipulative. Like a snake, he shows little or no signs of how he will bite and poison you to death. In this section, you should get equipping to understand and discern an Amnon type of man. You will be able to distinguish between a man who is serious and a man who wants to use and exploit you.

His Traits and Character

- The first thing you will notice about an Amnon type of man is he will not take "No" for an answer. As a woman you have to be very careful about a man who will not take no for an answer. Such men believe they deserve everything and that they are extra special and must have whatever they want, even if it's forbidden or inappropriate. As a woman you must understand that this sort of attitude is not a sign of the heroism of the "knight in shining armour", rather this is a sign of a potential abuser. It is a very frightful thing to be in a secluded place with a man who doesn't take no for an answer.

⅄ If you are in a relationship with him, he will force his ideas and plans on you because you are like his "property". Your opinions and requests will not be vital to him.

⅄ Amnon will not rest until he manages to uncover you and have sex with you. His mind is filled with lust and because he is a pathological liar, he will even convince himself that he loves you, yet true-love is not self seeking. He "loves" you only for sex and afterwards he will drop you faster than gravity and be on his way to find his next adventure.

⅄ He seems respectful and will treat you with courtesy in the beginning, he will wine and dine you and do everything so perfectly just to gain access to your trust and most importantly, your body.

⚼ You will know Amnon by the friends he has. His friends are rebellious, crafty, usually lacking piety and respect for women. Though he hides his character to you, you will surely see his character through his friends, for birds of a flock move together.

⚼ Amnon is a sweet talker, he will tell you "I can't sleep or I can't eat thinking of you." Indeed, he is right, he can't sleep nor eat because he is thinking of you! A wise woman considers why a man can't sleep nor eat, what is he thinking that's removing the peace of sleeping or appetite for eating. When love is pure, it doesn't take away appetite nor sleep, rather lack of sleep and appetite are linked with depression or stress. Lust takes away peace but real healthy love that springs from a pure heart gives peace of mind, joy and happiness.

⚼ Amnon preys on sweet, young and innocent women and after sleeping with you when he has finished with you, he will start making excuses to cut-off the friendship with you by playing reverse psychology on you. He will stop calling or texting you as often as he used to because he got what he wanted. His ways are similar to that of a psychopath in that he will put the blame on you by blaming you for why he is not texting you or calling you; this is all manipulation.

✠ Amnon does not have the Spirit of God in him therefore his judgements and solutions are of poor quality. His counsel comes from wicked influences, usually friends of corrupt minds. Do not trust his words but let his actions justify himself to you. He will say he's a Christian or loves God but his actions prominently repel what he is saying. He loves God but his conversations with you don't reflect Christ. He may also talk a lot about secular rappers, song and lyrics because that is what consumes His life rather than the Word of God. How can darkness and light have fellowship together? Daughter of God, let me make it clear to you that, there is no way that a man who consumes himself with God's presence and Word can delight in listening to music lyrics from secular music artists like Jay-Z and Eminem.

- There's no telling how deeply debased and crude Amnon's mind is. It is filled with all kinds of filth and lusts. He's dreaming and plotting all kinds of lustful things he's going to do to you once he gets to uncover you. This man is ungodly and will take great advantage on inexperienced or naive women.

- He acts very gentle, soft spoken and kind but truthfully he is violent and capable of beating up a woman or raping her; be alert around such type of men.

- He is a typical hypocrite. Amnon is the greatest masquerade you will ever encounter in your life. There is no fear of God in him, hence, his evil heart is unbounded from freely being a hypocrite. He will hide behind his nice car and clothes, he will hide behind his handsome smile, he will even hide behind his flawless prince charming attitude but yet he is wearing a mask.

- Like certain murderers, the family will be in shock to hear their son killed someone because they didn't see the signs. Likewise, Amnon is a somewhat of a good man in everyone's sight. This is because no one really knows him because he doesn't have close best friends but rather acquaintances and friends.

Evaluation

Now that you have seen the different traits and characters of the spirit of Jezebel, Athaliah, Delilah and Amon; what have you learnt from this chapter? I pray you can use this chapter to identify if those around you; you friends, family, colleagues and acquaintances are operating under the influence of any these spirits. Ask the Holy Spirit to open your eyes to identify those around you who are led by either one of these spirits. Say "Holy Spirit give me wisdom on how to deal and interact with (insert person), Holy Spirit by Your power, cut the cord of influence that they have on me and my life. Amen."

Sometimes, the people being used by this spirits can be close family members or people that you live with, as you have asked for wisdom in prayer, God will help you to deal with them. The Holy Spirit may lead you to fast or pray fervently or He may ask you to leave as the LORD did to Abraham in Genesis 12:1.

Moreover, it's very possible that you personally can begin to be used by either one of these spirits to influence or destroy someone else's life. For example, jealousy can open the door for a spirit of Jezebel to influence you to hurt someone else. I pray you can continue to use this chapter to access you own heart and actions. Perhaps you are trying to seduce other men or women like Delilah did? Are you trying to steal, kill and destroy other people's lives like Jezebel and Athaliah did because of bitterness, jealousy or envy? Are you behaving in the way that Amnon did by not having boundaries, goodness or purity in your heart in your friendships or relationship? If so, today you can repent and ask God to deliver you from everything that is causing you to allow these spirit to influence you for example envy. Begin by first repenting and then ask God to deliver you from envy by praying according to Psalm 51:10 saying, "Create in me a clean heart, O God, and renew a steadfast spirit within me in Jesus name, Amen. Remember to Continue speaking the word of God over yourself daily in order to combat evil thoughts from the enemy that want you to go back to being envious."

Conclusion

What have you learnt about yourself and about God ways and plans, from the 6 chapters in this book? What tools of encouragement have you taken with you to begin a new journey in your personal life, relationships and walk with God; with open eyes that see? I pray that every form of blindness you had was removed by the Blood of Jesus Christ as you read this book and that daily you will fill yourself with Jesus through His WORD which brings light, wisdom and fulfilment. I pray that every chain of imprisonment that was entangling you was broken by the anointing of God the Holy Spirit.

If you have not yet given your life to Jesus the Christ, you are missing out on real love, hope and peace that transcends all understanding. It's written in Romans 10.9 that "*if you confess with your mouth, "Jesus is LORD," and believe in your heart that God raised him from the dead, you will be saved.*"

Just believe in your heart today that Jesus is the Son of God and confess it with your

mouth. Say "Jesus I believe You are the Son of the living God, today be the LORD and God of my life and teach me Your ways daily by Your Spirit, fill me right now with Your Holy Spirit in Jesus name, Amen."

You are now a new person in Christ, forgiven and sanctified! Now purchase a bible in the NKJV, if you don't already have one and beginning with the book of John read all through it then Luke, Mark, Matthew and all the way to Revelations, then read from the book of Genesis up to the book of Matthew. Begin to study your bible daily to know who Jesus is and who you are in Him. Even if it means being secluded from the world and from your friends for a time, even if they mock you, believe me, knowing who you are first through knowing who Jesus is, is more important than anything in the world. Lastly, although there are many online bible teachings including bible study teachings that I personally do (via my youtube channel titled Dephne Madyara), I, however, strongly recommend that you find a good local church, ask your relatives or friends where they attend church and then start attending church services, bible studies and prayer meetings so that you can grow and fellowship with others.

The grace of our LORD Jesus Christ, the love of God and fellowship of the Holy Spirit be with you today and forever. Amen. God bless you.

In His service

Dephne Victorious Madyara

Dephne Madyara

Acknowledgements

I'd like to give special honour to my wonderful mother Elizabeth, my father Daniel and my step father Biton who all have been strong pillars of my life and are the most incredible and real parents anyone can ever have. I also want to thank my beloved Lloyd for his wisdom, humility, love and gentleness towards me and my ministry. Special thanks to my Pastors, Apostle Angie and Pastor Haziel for shepherding me in the right direction through the Word of God, encouragement and prayers. I also want to thank brother Maxwell Christian for his tremendous and timely help with this book. The LORD bless you all abundantly and I love you.

Referencing

www.bibligateway.com

www.blueletterbible.org

www.bible.cc

www.dictionary.reference.com

http://dephnevictorious.wordpress.com/

Sermon by Dr Myles Monroe called "Ladies, few things you must know before dating" - via www.youtube.com

Contact Author

Website: www.dephnemadyara.com

Twitter: @DephneMadyara

Facebook Page: https://www.facebook.com/dephnemadyar/

Instagram: https://www.instagram.com/dephnemadyara/

Printed in Great Britain
by Amazon

37136771R00145